"With her incredible second cookbook Ashley elevates the oil-free plant-based lifestyle with inspired and delicious recipes that will delight your family and guests alike!"

—KRISTEN HONG, author of *Fridge Love*

"Ashley proves that healthy food can be deliciously indulgent and satisfying with this book!"

—HANNAH SUNDERANI, creator of Two Spoons and bestselling author of *The Two Spoons Cookbook*

"This book is full of recipes that are absolutely divine and original, deeply satisfying, and perfect for supporting health in the most scrumptious way. It's a must-have book in every kitchen, regardless of dietary lifestyle."

—GINA FONTANA, creator of Healthy Little Vittles and author of *The Beginner's Guide to Gluten-Free Vegan Baking*

"Ashley shows you how to use whole-food ingredients to build the most magical meals. Her recipes incorporate the healthiest ingredients in genius (yet easy) ways. This book brings cozy plant-based meals into the home kitchen."

—MIYOKO SCHINNER, founder of Miyoko's Creamery

"This book is destined to become an essential and well-used cookbook for anyone looking to up their healthful plate without sacrificing flavor. Every recipe is foolproof and designed to take the stress and concern out of wholesome cooking."

—DUSTIN HARDER, host, chef, author, and creator of The Vegan Roadie

PLANT-BASED DELICIOUS

Healthy, Feel-Good
Vegan Recipes You'll Make
Again and Again

ASHLEY MADDEN
Creator of Rise Shine Cook and author of *The Plant-Based Cookbook*

PAGE STREET
PUBLISHING CO.

PAGE STREET
PUBLISHING CO.

First published in 2023 by
Page Street Publishing Co.
27 Congress Street, Suite 1511
Salem, MA 01970
www.pagestreetpublishing.com

Distributed by Macmillan, sales in Canada by The Canadian Manda Group.

27   26   25   24   23   1 2 3 4 5

ISBN-13: 9781645679820
ISBN-10: 1645679829

Library of Congress Control Number: 2022946898

Cover and book design by Rosie Stewart for Page Street Publishing Co.
Photography by Ashley Madden. Lifestyle Photography by Anne Allen Spencer.

Printed and bound in the United States

DEDICATED TO GEORGE.

My tiniest taste tester and the love of my life.

CONTENTS

INTRODUCTION

The distance between flavorful comfort food and plant-forward meals is much, much shorter than you might think. In other words, delicious, indulgent, satisfying foods can also be healthy.

Like really, really healthy.

If you haven't already experienced this, you'll discover throughout this cookbook that wonderful things happen when you substitute whole foods for processed ingredients.

I learned this over a decade ago when I started to prepare my own plant-based recipes. Lasagna, burgers, risotto, pizza. The flavors and textures were downright delightful and left nothing to be desired. The meals coming out of my kitchen seemed to combine what I once thought dissonant—food that was good for my body, pleasing to the belly and soothing to the soul. I savored every bite and wondered why I had waited so long to eat this way.

For me, it took a health crisis to reevaluate my own diet and lifestyle. I was diagnosed with multiple sclerosis in my twenties, and it had a domino effect. I gave up dairy and other animal products, started cooking for myself, drifted away from my profession as a pharmacist, became a holistic nutritionist and went to culinary school.

It changed my life.

And ever since, my heart has been devoted to making the foods we love, love us back.

Often "plant-based" conjures images of leafy greens and carrot sticks, totally wonderful vegetables, but these poster foods don't represent the abundant diet now well known as the plant-based diet—a diet built from whole grains, legumes, vegetables, fruit, nuts and seeds.

These nutritious foods can be used in countless ways to make mouthwatering, comforting meals. Scan the pictures in this book and skim through the recipes: This is what represents a modern, whole food, plant-based diet. Gone are the days of *healthy* being synonymous with *bland*. You won't have to convince yourself of anything, your taste buds will lead you through these outrageously flavorful and vibrant meals and food combinations.

These recipes flip the script and redefine, dare I say upgrade, comfort food. They're proof that family meals can be as nutritious and healthy as they are enjoyable and exciting. If you're looking to make the dinner table a happier, more wholesome, veg-friendlier, flavor-filled place, this cookbook will do just that.

Welcome to my plant-based kitchen, where a fresh and flavor-first approach to comfort food will change . . . everything!

Happy Cooking,

Ashley

NOTES FOR ALL RECIPES

Here are a few quick tips for cooking at home and following recipes. These are especially helpful if you're new to plant-based meal preparation or working with whole foods.

Oil-free sautéing. Sautéing without oil is easy. Simply add water or vegetable stock to the pan as you would oil and keep the heat at medium. Stir often and add more water or stock, a few tablespoons (about 30 ml) at a time as needed to prevent burning or sticking. I like to keep a glass, pitcher or measuring cup of water next to the stove. How much you use depends on how quickly it evaporates from the pan.

Soaking. Many of these recipes suggest soaking nuts and seeds before blending, which helps create a smooth and creamy texture and aids digestion. Soaking is ideal, but if you have a high-speed blender and are short on time, you can usually get away with skipping the soak. I share this with you so you can judge for yourself and do what suits your needs.

Chop first! If you like to take your time in the kitchen or find it hard to keep up with fast recipes, I suggest chopping, slicing and dicing all the veggies before you start cooking. If you're comfortable in the kitchen and are used to multitasking and keeping pace, feel free to prepare the veggies as they're needed.

Heat! Red pepper flakes are used in several of these recipes; remember that you can always adjust the amount to suit your needs and preferences. If you're not used to spicy foods, add conservatively or omit altogether.

Sodium. You can modify any added sodium in the form of sea salt or tamari as you see fit. In some recipes, I wait until the end to add the salt, and in others, it's added in the beginning or throughout, but you can always adjust to meet your needs.

Measuring flours. When measuring flours for baking, it's important to scoop the flour into measuring cups and level the cups with the straight edge of a butter knife. It's easiest to scoop the flour with the measuring cup but this will often lead to more flour than the recipe calls for. Weighing flours is the most accurate, but I'm guilty of using measuring cups on most occasions.

If you eat gluten. These recipes are gluten-free to accommodate those that follow a gluten-free diet, but they're made without overly fussy ingredients. If gluten is in your diet, you can replace gluten-free ingredients with gluten-containing ones you likely already have on hand. For instance, for any recipe that calls for gluten-free oats or a gluten-free bread, you can use regular oats or your favorite whole-grain bread; likewise, you can use whole wheat pasta for any other pasta listed. And finally, if you are fine with gluten, soy sauce or shoyu (which contain wheat) can generally be used instead of gluten-free tamari.

The comfort of cooking. The process of peeling, chopping, simmering and stirring does not need to be an arduous one. If we're open to the experience, it can be grounding, soothing and ultimately a crucial part of the comfort that good food can provide. The more we make food preparation, cooking and mindful eating a priority (I know it can be difficult), the sooner we'll feel like we're taking better care of ourselves and our families. Because we are. And that is the most comforting thing of all.

BUT FIRST, BREAKFAST (AND BRUNCH)

I feel the most comforted in the early morning hours. I like how morning seems to wrap around me like no other time of day and I feel the same about breakfast. Not racing-out-the-door breakfast but the kind you want to sit for. The kind you nibble on while the stove is busy and everyone's barefoot, lounging in pajamas. I give a lot of thought to that first meal because I am a breakfast lover.

These wholesome breakfast recipes range from the familiar and traditional, like Three-Grain Slow-Cooker Porridge (page 32), to the new and modern, such as Tofu Benedict Bowls with Corn Hollandaise and Spinach (page 27), but they all deliver on taste, nutrition and comfort.

Pour yourself something hot, throw on your favorite apron (or housecoat) and let's get cooking.

BLUEBERRY TEFF PANCAKES WITH LEMON

MAKES 12 PANCAKES ✿ NUT-FREE OPTION

1 cup (140 g) whole-grain teff flour

2 tbsp (19 g) coconut sugar (optional)

1½ tsp (7 g) baking powder

¼ tsp ground cinnamon

¼ tsp sea salt

1 medium-sized ripe banana

1 cup (240 ml) unsweetened almond milk or organic soy milk

2 tbsp (32 g) stirred almond butter or sunflower seed butter

Zest of 1 large lemon

1 tbsp (15 ml) fresh lemon juice

2 tsp (10 ml) pure vanilla extract

2 cups (290 g) fresh blueberries

FOR SERVING

Vegan yogurt (soy, nut or coconut)

Raw or toasted sliced almonds

Pure maple syrup

Pancakes make for good mornings, and this recipe is a pancake revival—nutty, fluffy, bursting with juicy berries and distinctively healthy—thanks to nutritious teff flour. These came about one Saturday morning when I ran out of the other typical pancake flours. Unwilling to give up my beloved pancakes, I experimented with some teff flour that I had hanging out in my pantry. The results were so delicious and so darn nourishing that this is now our Saturday morning tradition—lemony teff pancakes, lots of berries and a (big) oat milk matcha latte.

Teff, if you're not familiar, is the smallest grain on the planet, but despite being teeny tiny, it's packed with such nutrients as dietary fiber, iron and calcium. It's especially high in protein and offers all the essential amino acids. Teff flour can be found in most health food stores and online. Bob's Red Mill® is my preferred brand.

I like to serve these pancakes with a sprinkle of sliced almonds for crunch, a dollop of vegan yogurt for creaminess and a light drizzle of pure maple syrup for an extra touch of sweetness. My one-year-old loves them (the sugar-free version), too.

Preheat your oven to its lowest setting and line a large baking pan with parchment paper.

In a medium-sized bowl, combine the teff flour, coconut sugar (if using), baking powder, cinnamon and salt, and mix.

In a blender, combine the banana, milk, almond butter, lemon zest and juice and vanilla, and blend until completely smooth.

Pour the banana mixture into the dry ingredients and whisk together until no dry spots remain.

(continued)

BUT FIRST, BREAKFAST (AND BRUNCH)

Heat a large nonstick pan over low to medium heat. When the pan is hot, pour about ¼ cup (60 ml) of the batter into the pan. Give the pan a gentle shake to spread the batter a little. Drop five blueberries onto each pancake and cook over low heat for 3 to 5 minutes, or until the edges of the pancakes are cooked and bubbles form across the surface. Using a thin, nonscratch spatula, flip the pancake and cook for another minute or two. Place the pancakes on the prepared baking sheet and into the oven to keep warm. Repeat with the remaining batter and remember that the subsequent batches will cook a little faster. If the batter thickens and is no longer pourable, add a little bit more milk and whisk to loosen.

Serve the pancakes with a dollop of vegan yogurt and more blueberries, top with almonds and finish with a drizzle of maple syrup.

A GUIDE TO GOOD PANCAKES

- *Keep the pan over low to medium heat. If your pan is too hot, you run the risk of cooking the outside of the pancakes while the middle is undercooked. Slow and steady wins the pancake race.*

- *Be patient. Resist flipping too early. Wait until you see some bubbles form across the surface of the pancake and the center no longer looks wet.*

- *Use a good nonstick pan. If you want to make oil-free pancakes, the solution is to get a good-quality nonstick pan and use nonscratch utensils.*

- *Keep your pancakes warm before serving. Preheat your oven to the lowest setting; use your warming drawer if you have one.*

- *Whisk, then work. Such leavening agents as baking powder start to work right away and you want to benefit from the "fluff" factor they contribute. It's best to make the batter and get to work within 5 minutes of whisking.*

AVOCADO TOAST, SIMPLE SCRAMBLE AND MAPLE CARROT BAKON

MAKES 4 SERVINGS ⊛ NUT-FREE

SCRAMBLE

1 (14-oz [400-g]) package firm or extra-firm tofu

1 tbsp (4 g) nutritional yeast

½ tsp garlic powder

¼ tsp ground turmeric

Pinch of red pepper flakes (optional, if you like it with a little kick)

Pinch of freshly ground black pepper

½ tsp kala namak (black Indian salt) or sea salt

MAPLE BAKON

2 large carrots

2 tbsp (30 ml) tamari

1 tbsp (15 ml) pure maple syrup

1 tbsp (4 g) nutritional yeast

1 tsp smoked paprika

½ tsp garlic powder

½ tsp onion powder

Pinch of freshly ground black pepper

Over the years, "Just put it on toast" has become a speedy-meal slogan for our family. It's easy, convenient and familiar. But for a savory, feel-good breakfast, this avocado toast paired with a simple, might I add flawless, tofu scramble and topped with a mound of sweet and salty carrot ribbon bakon is perfection. You can choose your preferred toast—gluten-free bread, sourdough bread, Baked Buckwheat Bread (page 20) or skip the bread and use baked potatoes instead (see Note).

Start with the scramble: Give the block of tofu a squeeze over the sink to remove any excess water.

Crumble the tofu into a medium-sized bowl. Do this by holding the block over the bowl and breaking it into smaller pieces with your fingers. Add the nutritional yeast, garlic powder, turmeric, red pepper flakes (if using), pepper and kala namak, and mix to combine. Set aside until needed.

While the tofu is marinating, make the maple bakon: Peel the carrot into thick strips using a vegetable peeler; a Y-type peeler is the easiest to use. Lay the carrot on a cutting board, hold your hand steady and try your best to get thick, long strips. Wide, robust carrots are great for this. Once you start peeling into the fibrous core of the carrot, turn and peel the other side. You want about 2 full cups (150 g total) of carrot ribbons. Use the leftover fibrous cores in a veggie stock or chop into your next soup or salad.

In a medium-sized bowl, mix together the tamari, maple syrup, nutritional yeast, paprika, garlic and onion powders and black pepper, and add the carrot strips to the bowl. Toss with tongs or a fork until all the ribbons are covered.

(continued)

AVOCADO TOAST

2 avocados, pitted and peeled

Lemon wedge

4 thick slices of your favorite bread (see Notes for a nonbread option)

Heat a large nonstick pan over medium heat. Add the carrot bakon mixture, including all the liquid left in the bowl, and cook for about 3 minutes, tossing the carrot strips around with nonscratch tongs and adding just a tiny bit of water to loosen if they start to stick to the pan. They'll shrivel in size but still have bite. Transfer the carrot bakon to a clean bowl.

Carefully give your pan a wipe (it will be hot) to remove any stuck-on bits and return it to the stove. Heat over medium heat and add the tofu scramble mixture, including all its marinade. Cook, stirring often, for 5 to 6 minutes, or until the tofu has firmed up and any liquid in the pan has evaporated. If the tofu starts sticking, add a little water to help loosen.

Meanwhile, make your avocado toast: In a small bowl, mash the avocados, add a squeeze of lemon juice and mix until creamy.

When the scramble is done, turn off the heat and toast your bread. Layer each slice of bread with creamy avocado, then the tofu scramble and top with the maple bakon.

> ### NOTE
>
> *For a bread-free option, replace the bread with a baked potato or sweet potato. Bake the potato in the oven or a microwave, slice the potato open, fluff the insides and top with avocado, tofu scramble and maple bakon.*

NORDIC BIRCHER BOWLS

MAKES 4 TO 6 SERVINGS NUT-FREE OPTION

2 cups (180 g) gluten-free old-fashioned rolled oats

¾ tsp ground cinnamon

2 tbsp (26 g) chia seeds

¼ cup (36 g) whole or chopped almonds

¼ cup (35 g) pumpkin seeds

¼ cup (35 g) raisins

4 dried unsulfured apricots, diced

½ cup (60 g) unsulfured dried apple rings, diced

2½ cups (590 ml) unsweetened almond or organic soy milk, plus more if needed

2 tsp (10 ml) fresh lemon juice (optional)

1½ cups (345 g) unsweetened dairy-free plain yogurt (soy, coconut or cashew)

2 bananas, sliced

Bircher bowls, the original overnight oats, were developed by a Swiss physician, Dr. Bircher-Benner, in the early 1900s to help treat his patients. This version is on the heartier side and proves that an uncooked breakfast can still be satisfying and filling with a stick-to-your-ribs feel. The ingredients were thoughtfully chosen to provide a well-rounded, nutritious bowl. Immunity-boosting zinc from pumpkin seeds, blood-building iron from apricots, anti-inflammatory omega-3 fats from chia seeds . . . I could keep going! This wholesome bowl provides an array of essential vitamins and minerals, not to mention fiber and protein. I love to stir this together in a lidded container and eat it over a few days. It's perfect for overnight trips as well when you need an easy, comforting start to the day.

In a medium-sized bowl or a container with a lid, combine the rolled oats, cinnamon, chia seeds, almonds, pumpkin seeds, raisins, apricots, diced apple rings and milk, and mix. The milk should just cover the oats. Cover or secure the lid and place the bowl in the fridge overnight.

In the morning, stir in the lemon juice (if using) and divide the oat mixture among bowls. Serve with a generous dollop of yogurt and sliced banana.

NOTES

Try substituting a peeled and grated apple for the dried apple rings if you want a little extra sweetness and a different texture.

For a nut-free option, substitute sunflower seeds for the almonds.

To add some superfood power, add ¼ cup (25 g) of goji berries.

To make this Bircher bowl even creamier, replace ¾ cup (177 ml) milk with ¾ cup (172 g) vegan yogurt before soaking overnight.

If you want more protein, use soy milk instead of almond milk.

BAKED BUCKWHEAT BREAD WITH HOMEMADE SUNFLOWER SEED BUTTER

MAKES 1 LOAF · NUT-FREE

2 cups (360 g) whole buckwheat groats

3 tbsp (15 g) whole psyllium husk

1 cup (240 ml) water

2 tbsp (26 g) chia seeds

1 tbsp (14 g) baking powder

1¼ tsp (8 g) sea salt

1 tbsp (15 ml) pure maple syrup (optional)

½ cup (70 g) pumpkin seeds or sunflower seeds (optional)

Whole and modest buckwheat (a pseudograin related to rhubarb) makes a shockingly good bread. In my first cookbook, *The Plant-Based Cookbook*, I shared my "Amazing Multigrain Bread" made from oats, quinoa and buckwheat; it's one of the most popular recipes in the book, but I also received many requests for something similar that was oat- and quinoa-free. I heard you and here it is!

This loaf is simple yet superb. I highly suggest toasting the sliced bread and smearing it with dreamy sunflower seed butter (recipe follows) for a toast experience like no other. If you're making both simultaneously, toast the sunflower seeds first, then get the bread in the oven so you can work on the butter while the bread is baking.

Place the buckwheat groats in a medium-sized bowl and cover with 2 inches (5 cm) of water, cover the bowl with a clean dish towel and let the buckwheat soak for 4 hours or overnight.

When the soaking time is up, drain the buckwheat in a fine-mesh strainer. The liquid that runs off will be thick and goopy—this is normal—and will take a few minutes to drain. Once you think it's fully drained, give the strainer a shake and let the buckwheat drain for another minute.

Preheat the oven to 350°F (180°C) and line a standard loaf pan (8½ x 4½ x 2½ inches [21.5 x 11.5 x 6.5 cm]) with parchment paper so that the paper covers the bottom and hangs out over the two longer opposing sides. Set aside.

In a small bowl, mix together the psyllium husk and water and set aside for 5 minutes to thicken.

(continued)

In a food processor, combine the drained buckwheat, thickened psyllium mixture, chia seeds, baking powder, salt and maple syrup (if using). Process continuously until the buckwheat groats are no longer whole and the mixture is almost smooth.

Now, add the pumpkin seeds (if using) and pulse a few times to incorporate. Transfer the batter to the prepared loaf pan and gently smooth the surface with a spatula. Score the batter several times with a sharp knife and place the pan in the oven on the middle rack. Bake for 1 hour, or until the bread has pulled away from the pan and is firm to the touch.

After 1 hour of bake time, lift the loaf out of the pan by pulling on the overhanging parchment paper. If the loaf is in contact with the pan anywhere, make sure to loosen it with a thin spatula or knife so it doesn't stick. Place the loaf directly back on the oven rack and continue to bake for another 10 to 12 minutes, or until the sides of the loaf are dry to the touch and firm.

Transfer the loaf to a cooling rack to cool completely (this is important) before slicing. Keep the sliced bread in the fridge for up to 5 days or in the freezer for up to 3 months.

SUNFLOWER SEED BUTTER

MAKES 2½ CUPS  NUT-FREE

3 cups (402 g) raw sunflower seeds

1 tsp sea salt

2 tbsp (30 ml) pure maple syrup

Sunflower seed butter is a pantry staple I like to make from scratch. This way, I can control the ingredients. It's also cheaper than most bottled varieties. After making it once, you'll see that the seeds go on a journey, moving from dry and clumpy to smooth and creamy. It feels like (and kind of is) culinary magic. The maple syrup and salt balance the bitterness from the seeds and help bring out the roasted, earthy tones, but you can omit both if you prefer. Be sure to start with raw, unsalted sunflower seeds.

Preheat the oven to 350°F (180°C) and line a large baking sheet with parchment paper. Spread out the seeds on the prepared pan and bake for 10 minutes, or until golden and fragrant.

Remove the seeds from the oven, transfer them to a large plate and set aside until they are cool enough to handle.

Once cooled, place the toasted seeds in a food processor and process continuously. The sunflower seeds will go through several stages and textures before reaching a smooth and runny consistency. Keep processing and scraping down the sides of the processor until the sunflower butter is thick like a paste. At this point, add the salt and maple syrup and process again.

Just when you think it's about to get creamy, it will clump together again. Persevere because suddenly it will start to loosen and spin around in a creamy, dreamy swirl! The whole process can take up to 15 minutes. Let the sunflower seed butter cool in the processor container (it will be very hot) before transferring it to a glass jar. Keep in the fridge, covered, for up to 3 months.

VEGETABLE QUICHE WITH BUCKWHEAT CRUST

MAKES 6 TO 8 SERVINGS

CRUST

¾ cup (72 g) blanched almond flour

¾ cup (90 g) buckwheat flour

1 tsp sea salt

¼ cup (60 g) unsweetened applesauce

3 to 4 tbsp (45 to 60 ml) water

Quiche was a special meal my mom made during the holidays or when we had company coming, and I was always fascinated by its versatility and how it combined so many savory, seasonal foods into one delicious tart. It wasn't until I changed my diet that I considered making a quiche of my own and it's one of the first recipes I ever veganized. This one comes together quickly despite having a homemade crust. The simple crust has a faint sweetness, like my mom's. As with any good brunch recipe, you'll consider eating this quiche for lunch and dinner, too. If asparagus isn't available or in season, use sliced mushrooms or finely chopped broccoli instead.

Position the oven rack in the middle of the oven and preheat to 350°F (180°C).

Start with the crust: In a large bowl, mix together the flours and salt. Add the applesauce and 3 tablespoons (45 ml) of the water. Mix, using a spatula, until all the liquid is absorbed, then use your hands to knead the dough for about a minute. If it's too dry and crumbly, add up to another tablespoon (15 ml) of water. Shape the dough into a ball and let rest for couple of minutes.

Line an 8-inch (20.5-cm) round springform pan with parchment paper. Do this by tracing the insert of the springform pan onto parchment paper. Cut it out and fit it into the pan. Press the dough evenly into the prepared pan, starting from the middle and working outward to the edge of the pan (not up the sides). Using a fork, poke a few holes in the dough, place it in the oven and bake for 8 minutes. Remove from the oven and set aside. Keep the oven on.

(continued)

FILLING

1 (14-oz [400-g]) package firm tofu, drained

¼ cup (16 g) nutritional yeast

⅓ cup (40 g) chickpea flour

1 heaping tbsp (20 ml) stirred tahini

2 tbsp (30 ml) fresh lemon juice

1 tsp tamari

½ tsp ground turmeric

1 tsp onion powder

¾ tsp kala namak (black Indian salt) or sea salt

Pinch of freshly ground black pepper

1 medium-sized onion, finely diced

Pinch of sea salt

3 cloves garlic, minced

1 medium-sized bunch (about 10.5 oz [300 g]) asparagus, woody ends discarded, chopped into 1" (2.5-cm) pieces (see Notes if using another veggie instead)

2 cups (60 g) baby spinach

1 to 2 tomatoes, sliced into ¼" (6-mm) slices

Meanwhile, start the filling: Break the tofu into a few pieces and place in a food processor or high-speed blender along with the nutritional yeast, chickpea flour, tahini, lemon juice, tamari, turmeric, onion powder, kala namak and black pepper. Process or blend until combined and smooth. It should be thick but not lumpy. You can add a little bit of water, no more than a couple of tablespoons (about 30 ml), if needed, to assist the blending. Set aside.

In a large pan, sauté the onion with a few tablespoons (about 30 ml) of water and a pinch of salt for 5 to 7 minutes, adding water as needed and stirring to prevent burning. Now, add the garlic, asparagus (setting aside a few asparagus tips to garnish the top of the quiche) and spinach, and continue to cook for another minute. Turn off the heat.

Drain off and discard any excess liquid in the pan, then add the tofu mixture to the pan. Mix, using a nonstick spatula, until well combined. Transfer the quiche batter to the prepared springform pan and smooth out the surface. Press the sliced tomatoes and reserved asparagus tips gently into the top.

Bake, uncovered, for 40 to 45 minutes, or until the surface is golden and firm to the touch. Remove the quiche from the oven and let it cool for at least 10 minutes. The quiche will set as it cools.

Use a thin spatula to loosen the sides of the quiche from the pan and then remove the springform collar. Slice with a sharp knife, wiping the knife after each cut to get clean slices, and serve!

> NOTES
>
> *If using mushrooms instead of asparagus, follow the recipe as written but cook 10 ounces (280 g) of sliced mushrooms with the onions for 3 to 5 minutes, or until the mushrooms shrink and release their juices. Cook until the extra liquid is reduced and then add the spinach and continue as written.*
>
> *If using broccoli, follow the recipe as written but replace the asparagus with 2 cups (142 g) of finely chopped broccoli.*

TOFU BENEDICT BOWLS WITH CORN HOLLANDAISE AND SPINACH

MAKES 3 TO 4 SERVINGS NUT–FREE OPTION

TOFU

1 (14-oz (400-g]) package extra-firm tofu

3 tbsp (45 ml) fresh lemon juice

¾ tsp kala namak (black Indian salt) or sea salt

2 tbsp (8 g) nutritional yeast

Freshly ground black pepper

CORN HOLLANDAISE

¾ cup (120 g) diced yellow onion

1½ cups (195 g) frozen corn kernels

¼ tsp sea salt

¼ cup (35 g) raw cashews or sunflower seeds, soaked in hot water for 1 hour

1 tbsp (15 ml) fresh lemon juice

1 tsp white miso

1½ tsp (8 g) Dijon mustard

2 tsp (3 g) nutritional yeast

Pinch of cayenne pepper

¾ cup (175 ml) water, plus more if needed

This vibrant breakfast bowl is a personal favorite. The egglike tofu and creamy hollandaise sauce are a nod to the original Eggs Benedict, but here we're substituting protein-rich quinoa for the English muffins and adding a layer of sautéed spinach for the most nutritious and satisfying breakfast, brunch, lunch or even dinner. Frozen corn kernels are just brilliant in the hollandaise as they lend a touch of sweetness and a soft golden hue. Kala namak (black Indian salt) is essential for an egglike flavor, but you can use regular salt if you don't have any on hand. This recipe could even fit in the "At Home Gourmet" chapter.

First, marinate the tofu: Drain the tofu and slice the block into ½-inch (1.3-cm)-thick slabs. Depending on the shape of your block of tofu, you might have squares or rectangles. In a large, shallow dish, whisk together the lemon juice, kala namak, nutritional yeast and several grinds of black pepper. Place the tofu slices in the marinade, flipping the slices to coat all sides. Place in the fridge for 1 hour to marinate, flipping the tofu a couple of times during that time.

When the hour is almost up, preheat the oven to 375°F (190°C) and line a large baking sheet with parchment paper. Place the tofu slices on the prepared baking sheet, brush with any remaining marinade and bake for a total of 35 minutes.

Meanwhile, make the corn hollandaise: In a large sauté pan, sauté the onion and frozen corn (no need to defrost) with a couple of tablespoons (30 ml) of water and the sea salt for 7 to 10 minutes, stirring often, until the onion is translucent. Add more water, if needed, but you shouldn't need to add much as the corn will also release water as it defrosts. Once done, transfer to a high-speed blender.

(continued)

BOWL

1 cup (176 g) uncooked white quinoa

16 to 20 asparagus spears, woody ends discarded

11 oz (300 g) baby spinach (about 10 cups)

Sea salt and freshly ground black pepper

Squeeze of fresh lemon juice

2 tbsp (17 g) capers, drained

3 green onions, thinly sliced

Red pepper flakes (optional)

Drain the cashews, discarding the soaking liquid, and add them to the blender along with the lemon juice, miso, Dijon mustard, nutritional yeast, cayenne and water. Blend on high speed until completely smooth. Add more water and blend again, if needed, to achieve a pourable consistency. Set aside.

After the tofu has been in the oven for about 15 minutes, start the bowl: Cook the quinoa according to package directions. Once done, fluff with a fork, cover and set aside to keep warm.

When there are 10 minutes left on the tofu, move the tofu to one side of the pan and arrange the asparagus spears on the other side of the pan. Continue to bake for the remaining 10 minutes. If you have thicker spears, pop them in the oven a little earlier.

Finally, once everything is ready, cook the spinach: Place the spinach in the same pan that was used for the corn hollandaise, add a few tablespoons (about 30 ml) of water and a pinch each of salt and black pepper. Sauté for a minute, or until the spinach is wilted and bright green. Finish with a squeeze of lemon juice.

Now, it's time to assemble: Layer each bowl with warm quinoa, sautéed spinach and baked tofu, and drizzle with corn hollandaise. Tuck the asparagus neatly on the side and top it all off with capers, green onions and a sprinkle of red pepper flakes, if desired.

> NOTE
>
> *If you love this hollandaise sauce, see how I use it to make Cream of Corn Risotto (page 147).*

WEEKEND HASH BROWN CASSEROLE

3 lb (1.4 kg) Yukon Gold potatoes, peeled and diced into ¼″ to ½″ (0.6- to 1.3-cm) cubes (about 8 cups)

2 large yellow onions, diced

½ tsp sea salt, plus more for the pot of potatoes

3 cloves garlic, minced

8 oz (225 g) button mushrooms, diced

3 medium-sized kale leaves, stemmed and thinly sliced, or 3 cups packed (120 g) baby spinach

BÉCHAMEL SAUCE

2 cups (280 g) raw cashews, soaked in hot water for 1 to 3 hours

3 tbsp (45 ml) fresh lemon juice

1 tsp sea salt

1 tbsp (4 g) nutritional yeast

2½ tsp (13 g) Dijon mustard

1¾ cups (414 ml) water, plus more if needed

Creamy hash brown casserole—it was an essential potluck meal when I was growing up. This (much) healthier version is a recipe makeover that pairs a smooth cashew béchamel sauce with parboiled potatoes, nutrient-dense greens and meaty mushrooms.

After you've peeled and chopped the potatoes, place them in a large pot of cold water and set aside. This keeps the potatoes from browning and helps remove excess starch, which will improve texture.

In a large sauté pan, cook the onions with ½ tsp salt and ¼ cup (60 ml) water over low to medium heat for 15 to 20 minutes. Add more water, as needed, to prevent burning and stir often. We want the onions to be very tender and begin to darken in color. Next, add the garlic and mushrooms and cook for another 5 minutes, stirring often. Try to resist adding water as the mushrooms will eventually release their own juices. Finally, stir in the kale and turn off the heat.

Meanwhile, preheat the oven to 350°F (180°C). Add a good spoonful of salt to your pot of potatoes and bring the water to a boil. Once boiling, lower the heat to a rapid simmer. Simmer the potatoes for 5 minutes, or until just tender. Carefully drain them in a colander and then transfer them to a large bowl. Transfer the sautéed veggies to the bowl as well and set aside.

While the potatoes and the onions are cooking, make the béchamel sauce: Drain the cashews, discard the soaking liquid and place them in a high-speed blender with the lemon juice, salt, nutritional yeast, Dijon mustard and water. Blend on high speed for 1 minute, or until the béchamel is silky smooth. Reserve approximately ½ cup (120 ml) of the béchamel sauce; pour the rest into the bowl of potatoes and vegetables and mix well. Transfer the mixture to a 9 x 13-inch (23 x 33-cm) casserole dish. Spread the mixture evenly with a spatula, pushing it into the corners and smoothing out the surface. Cover the dish tightly with tinfoil and bake for 35 minutes. Then, remove the tinfoil, pour the reserved béchamel over the top, spread it evenly and bake, uncovered, for another 10 minutes, or until the top is golden. Remove from the oven and serve immediately.

THREE-GRAIN SLOW-COOKER PORRIDGE

1 cup (176 g) gluten-free steel-cut oats

¾ cup (135 g) whole buckwheat groats

½ cup (90 g) whole amaranth

8 cups (1.9 L) water

1½ tsp (4 g) ground cinnamon

½ tsp sea salt

⅓ cup (85 g) nut butter of choice (optional)

1 cup (240 ml) almond milk or dairy-free milk of choice, plus more if needed (optional)

Optional toppings: nuts or seeds, sliced banana, fresh berries, goji berries, raisins, pure maple syrup, chia seeds or hemp seeds

Porridge is the perfect opportunity to try new whole grains, as the cooking methods and times are flexible and very forgiving. This porridge trinity is my go-to: steel-cut oats, buckwheat and amaranth. The grains are slow-cooked overnight, making a cozy, chewy and wholesome breakfast bowl. Be generous and creative with your toppings; keep leftovers in your fridge and heat on the stove with an additional splash of nondairy milk.

Place the oats, buckwheat, amaranth, water, cinnamon and salt in a 4 quart (4 L) slow cooker. Set the slow cooker to low and cover. Cook for 7 to 8 hours overnight.

In the morning, give it a stir and mix in the nut butter (if using) to make it creamier. I like to add almond milk as well; adjust the amount of milk according to how thick or thin you like it.

Divide among bowls and top with your favorite toppings.

> ## NOTES
>
> *Here's a stovetop option in case you don't have a slow cooker.*
>
> *In a medium-sized bowl, combine the oats, buckwheat and amaranth and cover with 3 inches (7.5 cm) of water. Cover the bowl with a clean dish towel and let the grains soak overnight on the counter. In the morning, drain and rinse the grains in a fine-mesh sieve, then transfer to a heavy-bottomed soup pot.*
>
> *Add 7 cups (1.7 L) of water and the cinnamon and salt to the pot and bring to a boil. Once boiling, lower the heat and simmer, uncovered, for 30 to 40 minutes, stirring often. Add more water (or dairy-free milk), as needed. Once the grains are cooked, turn off the heat and let the porridge rest for 5 minutes. Stir in the nut butter and more milk, if needed.*
>
> *If you don't have amaranth, you can use an equal amount of buckwheat or steel-cut oats instead.*

GOOD MORNING WHOLE FOOD MUFFINS

1½ tsp (3 g) whole psyllium husk

¼ cup (60 ml) water

2¼ cups (216 g) gluten-free old-fashioned rolled oats, divided

1 cup (96 g) blanched almond flour

2 tbsp (26 g) chia seeds

2 tbsp (22 g) hemp seeds

2 tsp (9 g) baking powder

½ tsp baking soda

½ tsp ground cinnamon

¾ tsp sea salt

½ cup (75 g) raisins, chopped pitted dates, chopped dried apricots or dried cranberries

½ cup (50 g) walnuts, chopped

¼ cup (35 g) pumpkin seeds or sunflower seeds

1 cup (240 ml) unsweetened almond milk or organic soy milk

Zest of 1 lemon or orange

1 medium-sized ripe banana

¼ cup (60 ml) pure maple syrup

1 cup (100 g) peeled and grated carrot (about 1 medium-sized carrot)

¾ cup (100 g) peeled and grated Granny Smith apple (1 apple)

For days when a sit-down meal isn't happening, these hearty muffins are my breakfast on-the-go. They're made from actual whole foods—carrot, apple, banana, nuts, oats—and are studded with all kinds of delicious crunchy bits. I've discovered through lots of muffin trial and error that blending a portion of the oats with the other wet ingredients results in a mouthfeel and crumb that can't be achieved with oat flour alone. Grating the carrot and apple is also a great way to add moisture, a little sweetness and extra texture, resulting in a rustic, filling muffin. I've provided options for the seeds and dried fruit—choose the ones you love! You'll savor every nourishing bite.

Preheat the oven to 350°F (180°C). In a small bowl, whisk together the psyllium husk and water, and set aside for 5 minutes to thicken.

In a large bowl, mix together 1 cup (96 g) of the rolled oats, the almond flour, chia and hemp seeds, baking powder, baking soda, cinnamon, salt, raisins, walnuts and pumpkin seeds. Set aside.

In a blender, combine the remaining 1¼ cups (120 g) of rolled oats, milk, citrus zest, banana and maple syrup, and blend on high speed until smooth. Pour this mixture, along with the thickened psyllium mixture, into the bowl of dry ingredients, and mix until no dry spots remain. Fold in the grated carrot and apple.

Transfer the batter to a 12-well nonstick or silicone muffin pan; each muffin well will be full. I like to use my 3.25-ounce spring-release scoop (also known as a disher) to get a nice, rounded muffin. This is the equivalent of ⅓ cup (80 ml). If you don't have a nonstick pan, use muffin liners. Bake for 25 to 27 minutes, or until the muffins are almost firm to the touch and the middles look dry.

Remove the muffins from the oven and let cool in the pan for 15 minutes. Then, transfer them to a cooling rack to cool completely. The bottoms of the muffins will seem moist and dense, but they will set as they cool.

Keep these muffins in a sealed container on the counter for 2 days, in the fridge for up to 5 days or the freezer for up to 3 months.

ASHLEY'S FAVORITES

The journey of making this cookbook mirrors a time in my life when I, more than ever, am craving and needing comfort. I've just had a baby, the pandemic is lingering, I live in Taiwan and I am often homesick, sleep deprived and pretty much always hungry. I rely on nutritious meals to fuel, energize, inspire and, ultimately, comfort me. As I write, I'm wrapped in a knitted blanket, black beans are simmering on the stove and there's a bunch of fresh herbs on the counter waiting to be whizzed into a creamy pesto. George will wake any minute from his nap.

The handful of recipes in this chapter are ones that aren't so much related in terms of theme, course or ingredients, but ones that I connected with on a more personal level and have kept coming back to. These have become some of my favorites and I hope you enjoy them, too.

ROASTED ROOTS, GREENS AND SUNFLOWER MISO CREAM

MAKES 3 SERVINGS ✿ NUT-FREE

ROOTS AND GREENS

1 tbsp (2 g) finely chopped rosemary leaves from 2 (5″ [12.7-cm]) sprigs, or 2 tsp (3 g) dried

1 tbsp (3 g) fresh thyme leaves from about 1 medium-sized bunch of thyme, or 2 tsp (2 g) dried

1 medium-sized to large sweet potato, peel on or off, diced into ½″ (1.3-cm) pieces (2 heaping cups [300 g])

2 large carrots, peeled and diced into ½″ (1.3-cm) pieces (2 cups [260 g])

3 tbsp (45 ml) aquafaba (See Notes), or 2 tbsp (30 ml) fresh lemon juice, plus more for greens, divided

2 medium-sized purple beets, peeled and diced into ½″ (1.3-cm) pieces (2 heaping cups [300 g])

Sea salt and freshly ground black pepper

1 large bunch fresh greens, such as kale, Swiss chard or bok choy—whatever is local and fresh and not too delicate, roughly chopped

This is a recipe where the whole is greater than the sum of its parts—separately, the components exude simplicity, but together, they feel sophisticated. It's an earthy but refined combination I retreat to in the fall and winter months when root vegetables abound. Beets, carrots and sweet potatoes are transformed in the oven where their sugars caramelize, creating delightful flavor and texture, while tempeh and greens are simmered and steamed in a pan. Everything is tied together with a tantalizing cream sauce that I could (and sometimes do) eat with a spoon. Use any leftover sauce as a salad dressing or vegetable dip.

Make the roots and greens: Preheat the oven to 425°F (220°C) and line a large baking sheet with parchment paper. In a small bowl, stir together the rosemary and thyme leaves.

In a large bowl, combine the sweet potato and carrots and toss with 2 tablespoons (30 ml) of the aquafaba or 1 tablespoon (15 ml) of the lemon juice. Sprinkle a little more than half of the rosemary and thyme mixture onto the veggies and toss again. Transfer to one side of the baking sheet.

Now, place the beets in the same bowl and toss with the remaining tablespoon (15 ml) of aquafaba or lemon juice, then the remaining rosemary and thyme, and spread them out on the other side of the baking sheet. We're tossing the beets separately to prevent everything from turning purple.

Season all the veggies with a sprinkle of salt and a few grinds of pepper and rearrange them so they're in a single layer. Roast in the oven for 30 to 35 minutes, flipping halfway through, or until all the veggies are fork-tender.

(continued)

SUNFLOWER MISO CREAM

¾ cup (109 g) raw sunflower seeds

1 tbsp (16 g) white miso

2 tsp (10 ml) pure maple syrup

1 large clove garlic, crushed and peeled

Juice of ½ lemon

1 tsp tamari

¾ cup (175 ml) water, plus more as needed

TEMPEH

1 (8-oz [225-g]) package tempeh, diced into ½" (1.3-cm) cubes

2 tbsp (30 ml) tamari

While the veggies are roasting, make the sunflower miso cream: In a large, dry skillet, toast the sunflower seeds over medium heat for 6 to 8 minutes, or until golden and fragrant. Remove the seeds from the heat and transfer them directly to a blender. Add the miso, maple syrup, garlic, lemon juice, tamari and water to the blender, and blend until completely smooth. Add more water to thin, if needed. You want a pourable but thick sauce, like a cream. Pour into a jar or container and set aside.

When the root veggies have about 10 minutes left, cook the tempeh. Place the tempeh in a medium-sized bowl and toss with the tamari until the tempeh has absorbed all the liquid. Then, transfer to the same skillet used to toast the sunflower seeds. Cook over medium heat, stirring often, for 5 to 6 minutes, or until browned. Add water, a couple of tablespoons (about 30 ml) at a time, as needed, to prevent burning.

Next, push the tempeh to one side of the pan and place the fresh greens on the other side. Add a couple of tablespoons (about 30 ml) of water and cover the pan. Here, we're steaming the greens for a couple of minutes until vibrant and just starting to wilt. Remember that the more fibrous the green, the longer the steaming time. Remove the cover, let any water cook off and add a squeeze of lemon juice to the greens. Remove from the heat.

Now, it's time to assemble. Spoon the roasted veggies, tempeh and greens into bowls in sections or all mixed together. Drizzle with creamy sunflower miso sauce and serve.

NOTES

Feel free to substitute another sauce for the sunflower miso cream if you have one already made in your fridge, or try this recipe without any sauce at all! I've made this combination several times when I've wanted a simple meal.

Aquafaba is the liquid in a can of chickpeas. It has a unique combination of protein and carbohydrates and is excellent at replacing oil and egg whites. I like using it on roasted vegetables as it coats well and keeps the veggies from drying out.

STICKY TERIYAKI CAULIFLOWER BOWLS WITH EDAMAME

BOWL

1 medium-sized head cauliflower (5 to 6 cups [500 to 600 g] florets)

½ cup (80 g) brown rice flour, plus more if needed

½ cup (120 ml) water, plus more if needed

¾ cup (132 g) uncooked white quinoa

1½ cups (222 g) frozen shelled edamame

This was my answer to a Friday night craving—it's a flavor bomb of a bowl. The cauliflower is baked in the oven, tossed with a finger-licking sweet-salty-sour sauce and served with warm fluffy grains and mild edamame. The drizzle of tahini is the perfect finish. I suggest first getting the cauliflower in the oven and then working on the other components. In terms of nutrition, this bowl has it all: complete protein, complex carbohydrates and antioxidant-packed cauliflower. You can make this sticky cauliflower on its own and serve as a snack or appetizer, too.

Preheat the oven to 425°F (220°C) and line a large baking sheet with parchment paper.

Start the bowl: Cut the cauliflower into 1½-inch (4-cm)-wide florets and set aside.

In a large bowl, whisk together the brown rice flour and water. The consistency should be thick like pancake batter. Add the cauliflower to the bowl and toss until all the florets are coated. If the batter is too thin and running off the florets, add another tablespoon (10 g) of rice flour and toss again. If it's too thick, add a bit of water and toss again.

Spread out the cauliflower in a single layer on the prepared pan and roast in the oven for 25 minutes.

Meanwhile, cook the quinoa according to the package directions. Once done, fluff with a fork, re-cover and set aside.

(continued)

STICKY SAUCE

¼ cup (60 ml) low-sodium tamari

¼ cup (60 ml) pure maple syrup

1 tbsp (15 ml) vinegar-based hot sauce (e.g., Frank's RedHot®)

1 tbsp (15 g) tamarind paste

1 tbsp (15 ml) tomato paste

2 tsp (10 ml) ginger juice (see page 133 for how to make ginger juice)

1 large clove garlic, minced

1 tsp arrowroot starch

1 tbsp (15 ml) water

FOR SERVING

3 tbsp (45 ml) stirred tahini

3 to 4 tbsp (45 to 60 ml) water

2 tbsp (16 g) black or white sesame seeds

3 green onions, thinly sliced

Next, bring a small pot of water to a boil. Once boiling, turn the heat to low, add the edamame and simmer, uncovered, for 3 to 4 minutes. Drain, set aside and cover to keep warm.

Now make the sticky sauce. In the same pot as you used for the edamame, combine the tamari, maple syrup, hot sauce, tamarind paste, tomato paste, ginger juice and garlic. Bring to a gentle simmer over low heat. In a small bowl, whisk together the arrowroot starch and water; this is called a slurry. Pour the arrowroot slurry into the pot and simmer over low heat, whisking, until thickened. The sauce should easily coat the back of a spoon. Remove the sauce from the heat.

After 25 minutes, the cauliflower should be just fork-tender. Remove the cauliflower from the oven and transfer it to a large bowl, reserving the prepared baking sheet. Pour the thickened sticky sauce over the cauliflower and toss with a silicone spatula until all the cauliflower florets are coated.

Spread out the cauliflower again on the baking sheet and return it to the oven for another 6 to 8 minutes.

When ready to serve, place the tahini in a small bowl, add 3 tablespoons (45 ml) of water and whisk. Keep adding water until it reaches a pourable consistency.

Now, assemble the bowls: Layer each bowl with cooked quinoa, edamame, sticky cauliflower and a drizzle of tahini sauce, and sprinkle with sesame seeds and green onion.

> ## NOTE
>
> *Tamarind paste is made from the fruit or pods of the tamarind tree. It's thick and dark, like molasses, tangy and very sour. It's a great addition to marinades and sauces. You can find tamarind paste at most health food stores and online. I use it again in the Pad Thai–Inspired Noodles with Tempeh and Broccoli (page 74).*

SLOW-COOKED BLACK BEANS WITH ALMOND CILANTRO PESTO AND CORN CHIPS

MAKES 4 TO 6 SERVINGS   NUT-FREE OPTION

BEANS

1⅓ cups (290 g) dried black turtle beans

8 to 10 large cloves garlic, crushed and peeled

1 large red onion, thinly sliced

6 cups (1.4 L) water, plus more if needed

¾ tsp sea salt, or to taste

1½ tsp (8 ml) red wine vinegar

Juice of ½ lime

This is one of the rare exceptions where I don't soak dried beans before cooking them. Here, we're skipping the soak to preserve the beautiful inky black color. The slow cook ensures the beans are cooked throughout and encourages the onion and garlic to melt into the pot. Preparing the beans takes a little time but barely any effort, and the results are superb. When paired with an herbaceous pesto and crunchy homemade corn chips, this makes a satisfying meal with many serving options or a unique snack board. If you aren't a fan of cilantro, use fresh mint or basil in the pesto instead and see the Notes for a pesto alternative. Look for authentic corn tortillas made with masa harina (corn flour), water and salt. The length of time to cook the beans will ultimately depend on the age of your beans. Old beans take longer, and some won't cook at all. It's best to buy fresh dried beans if you're not sure how long the beans have been in your pantry.

Make the beans: Pick through the beans and discard any discolored or misshapen ones. Rinse the beans and place them in a large, heavy-bottomed pot. Add the garlic, red onion and water. Bring to a boil and then lower the heat to a simmer. Simmer, covered, for 90 minutes, stirring occasionally. After 90 minutes, remove the cover and simmer for another 30 to 40 minutes, or until the beans are thick and creamy. Add more water, ½ cup (120 ml) at a time, if all the liquid cooks off before the beans are cooked through.

Once the beans are tender, add the salt, vinegar and lime juice. Stir and taste, and reseason with salt, if needed. Turn off the heat and cover until needed.

(continued)

TORTILLAS

8 (5″ [12.5-cm]) corn tortillas, cut into quarters

CILANTRO AND ALMOND PESTO

1 cup (145 g) whole almonds

Leaves and tender stems only from 2 bunches cilantro (about 2 packed cups [50 g])

2 cloves garlic, crushed and peeled

3 tbsp (45 ml) fresh lemon or lime juice

½ tsp sea salt, or to taste

½ avocado, pitted and peeled (optional)

⅓ cup (80 ml) water to thin, plus more as needed

Toast the tortillas: While the beans are simmering, preheat the oven to 375°F (190°C) and place the corn tortillas on a sheet pan. Bake for 10 to 15 minutes, or until golden. Remove the tortillas from the oven and set aside. They'll harden as they cool.

When the beans are almost ready, make the pesto: In a food processor, combine the almonds, cilantro, garlic, lemon juice, salt and avocado, and process until the almonds are crumbly. Scrape down the sides of the processor, add the water and process again continuously until creamy with some texture. Add more water, if needed, until the mixture is a little loose but not watery.

Scoop the hot beans into a serving bowl and serve them on a platter with corn tortilla chips and a side of the pesto. You can also serve this in individual bowls with beans on the bottom, pesto on top and chips on the side.

NOTES

If gluten isn't an issue, you can use whole wheat wraps and follow the same procedure for making chips.

For a nut-free option, use sunflower seeds instead of almonds in the pesto.

If you want a less creamy pesto, skip using the avocado.

OTHER SERVING IDEAS

Use these slow-cooked beans as the filling for your next taco or burrito and pair with the pesto or Cashew Sour Cream (page 120) and fresh veggies.

Serve these beans hot with just-cooked brown rice and steamed vegetables.

Serve the beans inside a baked potato topped with avocado.

GUACAMOLE (OPTIONAL)

MAKES 4 TO 6 SERVINGS

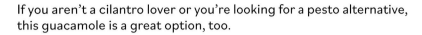

2 avocados, pitted and peeled

¼ small red onion, finely minced

1 tablespoon (15 ml) fresh lime juice

1 large clove garlic, minced

¼ teaspoon sea salt, plus more to taste

If you aren't a cilantro lover or you're looking for a pesto alternative, this guacamole is a great option, too.

Scoop the avocado flesh into a medium-sized bowl and add the red onion, lime juice, garlic and salt. Mash until the avocado is creamy but still has texture. Taste and reseason with salt and/or lime juice.

47

BROWN RICE POUTINE WITH MISO GRAVY

MAKES 3 LARGE BOWLS NUT-FREE OPTION

BOWL

1½ cups (270 g) uncooked long-grain brown rice

2 tbsp (30 ml) brown rice vinegar or regular rice vinegar, plus more for serving

1 (14-oz [400-g]) package extra-firm tofu, drained and cut into ½″ (1.3-cm) cubes

1 tbsp (10 g) brown rice flour

2 tbsp (8 g) nutritional yeast

½ tsp sea salt

¼ tsp freshly ground black pepper

3 cups (90 g) baby spinach

1 large carrot, cut into matchsticks

½ English cucumber, cut into matchsticks or thinly sliced

3 green onions, thinly sliced on a bias

¼ cup (36 g) raw or toasted sliced almonds

This is an Asian-inspired bowl that, although vastly different, gives a little nod to Canada's signature dish. Brown rice is layered with lightly battered tofu and crisp veggies, then smothered in a shiitake and miso gravy. The umami gravy, so good it's drinkable, comes together quickly, and if you start by cooking the rice and prepping the vegetables, you'll be sitting at the table in under an hour. I especially love how this bowl balances cooked and raw elements while including all the plant-based food groups.

Start the bowl: First, cook the brown rice according to the package directions. Once done, fluff with a fork, stir in the brown rice vinegar and set aside, covered, until needed.

Meanwhile, preheat the oven to 400°F (200°C) and line a baking sheet with parchment paper.

Place the cubed tofu in a bowl. It should still be damp from the water in its package, which will help the coating stick. In a separate small bowl, mix together the brown rice flour, nutritional yeast, salt and pepper. Sprinkle this over the tofu and toss until all the tofu is coated. Transfer to the prepared baking sheet and bake for 25 minutes, or until golden.

(continued)

MISO GRAVY

7 oz (200 g) shiitake mushrooms, thinly sliced

3 large cloves garlic, thinly sliced

2 tbsp (32 g) white miso

2 tbsp (30 ml) tamari

1 rounded tbsp (18 g) stirred almond butter

1 tbsp (4 g) nutritional yeast

1½ cups (355 ml) low-sodium vegetable stock

1 tsp vinegar-based hot sauce, plus more for serving

4 tsp (12 g) arrowroot starch

While the tofu is baking and the rice is simmering, make the miso gravy: In a medium-sized pot, cook the mushrooms with a couple of tablespoons (about 30 ml) of water over medium heat, stirring often for 3 to 5 minutes, or until they start releasing their juices. Now, add the garlic and cook for another 30 seconds. You can add small amounts of water if the garlic or mushrooms are sticking, but the mushrooms should release enough liquid. Turn off the heat.

In a blender, combine the miso, tamari, almond butter, nutritional yeast, stock, hot sauce and arrowroot starch, and blend until smooth. Pour the mixture into the pot containing the mushrooms and garlic and bring to a gentle simmer over low heat.

Simmer, stirring occasionally, for a few minutes until thickened. Be careful not to bring the gravy to a boil as this can "break" the consistency created by the arrowroot starch. Turn off the heat and cover the pot to keep the gravy warm.

Now, it's time to assemble: Layer each bowl with brown rice, a handful of spinach (the heat from the rest of the components will soften the spinach) and baked tofu, and pour the hot gravy over everything. Next, stack the carrot, cucumber and green onions on top. Garnish with sliced almonds and serve with additional hot sauce and brown rice vinegar.

> NOTES
>
> *For a nut-free option, you can substitute tahini or sunflower seed butter for the almond butter.*
>
> *Use different mushrooms to get a slightly different flavor. Oyster and cremini work well too.*
>
> *The baked tofu in this recipe is how we make tofu most of the time. I like to pair it with steamed veggies and cooked grains. One of my recipe testers suggested making the tofu by itself with a dipping sauce—brilliant! Try it with the Ranch Dressing on page 153 or the Sunflower Miso Cream on page 40.*

CREAMY CAULIFLOWER CURRY WITH CHERRY TOMATOES AND CHICKPEAS

MAKES 4 SERVINGS

½ cup (65 g) chopped carrot (1 small carrot)

1 cup (133 g) peeled and chopped sweet potato (1 small sweet potato)

¼ cup (38 g) chopped yellow onion (¼ onion)

1½ cups (285 g) uncooked brown rice

1 tbsp (6 g) whole cumin seeds

1 tbsp (5 g) whole coriander seeds

2 tsp (4 g) whole fennel seeds

3 large cloves garlic, crushed and peeled

1 (¾" [2-cm]) knob fresh ginger, peeled

¼ cup (64 g) stirred almond butter or all-natural peanut butter

½ tsp ground turmeric

Pinch of red pepper flakes, or to your preference

¾ tsp sea salt, or to taste

A few grinds of black pepper

2½ cups (590 ml) vegetable stock

Curry meets African nut butter stew in what we consider one of our favorite meals. The blended sauce, made from whole toasted spices and steamed veggies, is simmered with cauliflower and cherry tomatoes until the tomatoes break down and the sauce thickens. When I'm in the mood for heat, I add a little, or even a lot, of red pepper flakes. Feel free to make it as spicy as you like or omit the red pepper flakes completely. You can easily make the sauce ahead of time for faster dinner prep. The nut butter is prominent in building the flavor, so note that the taste will shift depending on which one you choose.

Fit a steamer basket into a large pot and fill the pot with water to just below the basket. Bring to a boil. Once boiling, place the carrot, sweet potato and onion in the basket and cover. Steam the veggies for 10 to 15 minutes, or until all are very tender.

Meanwhile, cook the brown rice according to the package directions. Once cooked, fluff with a fork and set aside, covered, until needed.

While the veggies are steaming and the rice is cooking, combine the cumin, coriander and fennel seeds in a large sauté pan and toast over medium heat for 2 to 3 minutes, or until fragrant and they just start to pop. Remove from the heat and transfer the seeds to a high-speed blender. You'll use the pan again.

Add the garlic, ginger, nut butter, turmeric, red pepper flakes, salt, black pepper and vegetable stock to the blender as well.

(continued)

CREAMY CAULIFLOWER CURRY WITH CHERRY TOMATOES AND CHICKPEAS

5 cups (500 g) bite-sized cauliflower florets (from 1 medium-size to large head)

2 cups (300 g) cherry tomatoes, any large ones cut in half

1½ cups (255 g) cooked or canned chickpeas, drained and rinsed

2 tbsp (30 ml) fresh lemon juice

Optional addition: 1 to 2 cups (30 to 60 g) baby spinach or (67 to 134 g) finely chopped kale

When the veggies are tender, remove the steamer basket from the pot and transfer the cooked veggies to the blender. Blend on high speed until the sauce is completely smooth. Set aside.

Place the cauliflower and tomatoes in the same large sauté pan as used for the spices and sauté with a few tablespoons (about 30 ml) of water for 5 minutes, or until the tomatoes start to soften a little. Add more water, if needed, to prevent burning. Pour in the blended sauce and bring to a simmer. Cover and simmer for 15 minutes. Then, remove the cover and break the tomatoes, using the back of a wooden spoon. They should easily break open. Be sure to break them away from you to avoid splashing yourself with the hot tomato juice!

Add the chickpeas and continue to simmer, uncovered, for another 10 to 15 minutes, or until the sauce has thickened and the cauliflower is fork-tender. Stir in the lemon juice and spinach (if using). Taste and reseason with salt and black pepper, as needed.

Spoon the rice onto plates or into bowls and top with the cauliflower curry.

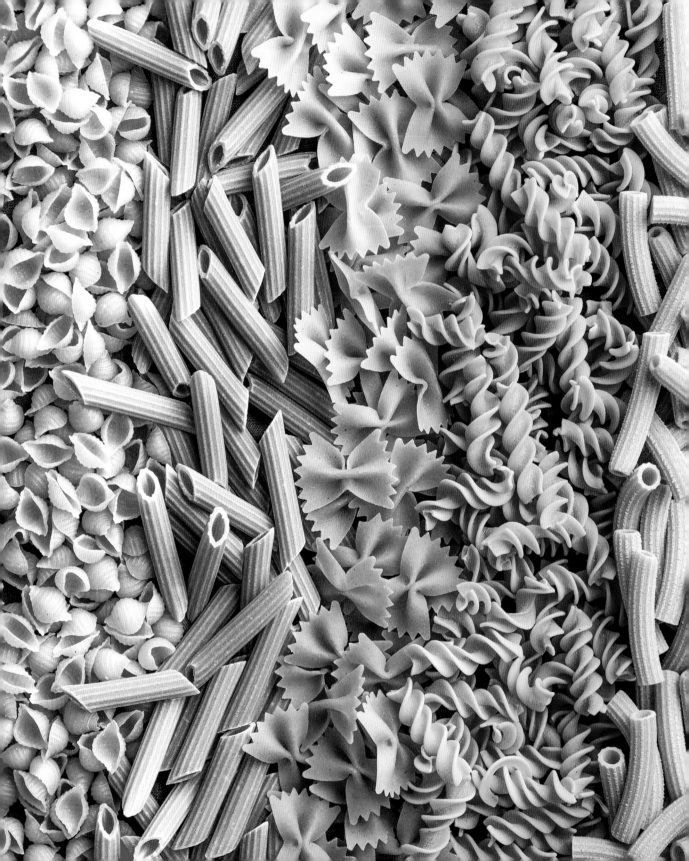

PASTA PLEASE: PERFECT POTS OF PASTA AND NOODLES

Today, it's easy to find a pasta or noodle that suits your needs—lentil, chickpea, brown rice, corn, quinoa, green pea . . . the list goes on and on! I've used a variety throughout this chapter and, for the most part, they're interchangeable. You'll also notice that I love slipping cruciferous veggies and greens of any kind into a pasta recipe. Nothing gives me more peace of mind than knowing a pot of tangly noodles is packed with nutrition.

There's a pasta for every occasion, too. Mixed Mushroom Lasagna with Kale and White Bean Ricotta (page 59) for a crowd, One-Pot Tuscan Pasta (page 70) for the busiest of weeknights, and Mac 'n' Cauli Cream (page 69) when you need to get some veggies into mouths (I have a toddler; this is a popular one for me).

Most of the sauces in this chapter are made with whole foods, which can dry out pasta if left sitting. I always suggest only dressing as much pasta as you're going to serve.

SPAGHETTI AND BEET BALLS

MAKES 40 TO 44 BEET BALLS; WITH SAUCE AND PASTA, SERVES 4 (WITH LEFTOVER BEET BALLS)

BEET BALLS

¾ cup (135 g) uncooked long-grain brown rice

¾ cup (75 g) walnuts

1½ cups (225 g) peeled and chopped purple beet (1 to 2 medium-sized beets)

½ cup (75 g) roughly chopped red onion

1½ cups (258 g) cooked or canned black beans, drained and rinsed

½ cup (50 g) gluten-free oat flour

3 tbsp (12 g) nutritional yeast

2 tsp (4 g) dried basil

1 tsp dried oregano

½ tsp red pepper flakes

2 tbsp (30 ml) red wine vinegar

2 tbsp (30 ml) tomato paste

1 tsp sea salt

Admittedly this recipe started out as just a name . . . I loved the snappy ring of spaghetti and *beet* balls. It's since become a family meal we look forward to. I keep a secret stock of beet balls in the freezer for those rushed evenings when I want a hurried but homemade meal. I say secret because my husband, Bernard, eats these beet balls like they're candy. Feel free to use your preferred marinara, but I've included my multipurpose house marinara here if you want to give it a go. The beet balls require cooked brown rice, which I like to make ahead of time so it's cool enough to handle. The recipe yields a lot of beet balls, so you'll have leftovers.

Make the beet balls: First, cook the rice according to the package directions. Once it's done, fluff with a fork and cover for another 5 minutes. Then, remove the cover and let the rice cool for 20 minutes before you start the rest of the recipe.

Preheat the oven to 350°F (180°C) and line a large baking sheet with parchment paper. If you have a small oven or don't have a large baking sheet, you'll need two baking sheets.

In a food processor, process the walnuts until crumbly. Transfer to a large bowl. Add the beets and onion to the food processor and process until finely chopped. The pieces of onion and beet should be about the size of a grain of rice. Transfer to the bowl that contains the walnuts.

Now, place the black beans, oat flour, nutritional yeast, basil, oregano, red pepper flakes, vinegar, tomato paste and salt, plus the cooked rice in the food processor and process until well combined and the black beans and rice grains are no longer whole. Add to the bowl that contains the beet mixture. Mix well. It will be thick and sticky with a little bit of texture.

(continued)

MY HOUSE MARINARA (OR USE 2 CUPS [475 ML] OF YOUR PREFERRED MARINARA)

1 cup (150 g) diced red onion

3 cloves garlic, minced

½ tsp dried oregano

Pinch of red pepper flakes (optional)

2 tbsp (30 ml) tomato paste

2 (15-oz [425-g]) cans tomato sauce or passata

¼ tsp sea salt, or to taste

1 tsp coconut sugar

1 tsp red wine vinegar

Handful of fresh basil, or ½ tsp dried

Freshly ground black pepper

PASTA

12 oz (340 g) dried brown rice spaghetti

¼ cup (18 g) Italian Parmesan (page 69) or preferred vegan Parmesan (optional)

Using a ¾-ounce spring release scoop (about 2 tablespoons [30 ml]), scoop out the mixture, form it into a ball and gently lay it on the prepared pan. Slightly wet hands will make the rolling process easier if you're not using a spring-release scoop.

Repeat with the remaining mixture, keeping about ½ inch (1.3 cm) between each ball, if possible. Depending on the size of your pan, it will likely be crowded; this is okay. Bake for 60 minutes, or until slightly firm; no need to flip. Remove from the oven and let the beet balls cool for 10 minutes. They'll set as they cool.

While the beet balls are in the oven, make the marinara (if not using a jarred marinara): In a medium-sized pot, sauté the onion with a few tablespoons (about 30 ml) of water for 5 to 7 minutes. Add water, as needed, to prevent burning. Now, add the garlic, oregano, red pepper flakes (if using) and tomato paste, and cook for another couple of minutes, stirring, until the tomato paste darkens in color. Next, add the tomato sauce, salt, coconut sugar and vinegar, and bring to a low heat. Simmer, partially covered, for 15 minutes, or until thickened. Transfer the sauce to a blender, add the basil and blend until completely smooth. Pour the marinara back into the pot and cover to keep warm.

When the marinara and beet balls are almost ready, make the pasta according to the package directions for al dente. Once the pasta is cooked, drain well in a colander and add back to the pot. Pour in the marinara and toss with tongs. Divide the pasta among plates or bowls and top with beet balls and the Parmesan(if using).

MIXED MUSHROOM LASAGNA WITH KALE AND WHITE BEAN RICOTTA

MAKES 9 SERVINGS

WHITE BEAN RICOTTA

2 cups (280 g) raw cashews, soaked in hot water for 1 to 3 hours

1½ cups (273 g) cooked or canned navy or (384 g) cannellini beans, drained and rinsed

3 tbsp (45 ml) fresh lemon juice

1 large clove garlic, crushed and peeled

¾ tsp sea salt

1 cup (240 ml) water

Large handful of fresh basil leaves

Lasagna is my first thought when I want to entertain a group with different preferences. It's a meal I'm excited to serve and thrilled to eat. Usually, I like to make a scrappy lasagna with all kinds of veggie odds and ends, but this one was inspired by an abundance of mushrooms I had on hand. I tossed in some sun-dried tomatoes and fresh kale, and what resulted was an incredibly filling meal with big flavor. The protein-rich bean ricotta, conveniently made mostly from pantry ingredients, is exceptional, easy to make and does wonderful things in the oven. When it's all layered between sheets of lasagna, it's a delicious feast.

First, make the ricotta: Drain the cashews, discarding the soaking liquid, and place them in a high-speed blender. Add the beans, lemon juice, garlic, salt and water. Blend until completely smooth. Use your tamper to assist the blending. Finally, add the basil and pulse until the ricotta is flecked with green and no whole basil leaves are visible. Set aside.

(continued)

VEGGIE FILLING AND PASTA

¼ cup packed (25 g) sun-dried tomatoes (not the kind packed in oil)

1 large yellow onion, diced

¼ tsp sea salt

Pinch of red pepper flakes

3 cloves garlic, minced

8 oz (225 g) cremini or portobello mushrooms, diced

8 oz (227 g) button mushrooms, diced

1 large bunch curly or lacinato kale, stemmed and chopped (about 3 packed cups or 7 oz [200 g])

1 tbsp (15 ml) fresh lemon juice

Several grinds of black pepper

4½ cups (1 L) jarred vegan marinara, or 2 batches My House Marinara (page 58)

12 to 14 oven-ready brown rice lasagna noodles

Next, move on to the filling: In a small bowl, soak the sun-dried tomatoes for 15 minutes in just enough water to cover. Meanwhile, preheat the oven to 375°F (190°C). In a large sauté pan, sauté the onion with ¼ cup (60 ml) water and the salt for 7 to 10 minutes, or until soft and translucent. Add more water, as needed, to prevent burning.

Now, add the red pepper flakes, garlic and mushrooms to the pan and continue to sauté over medium heat until the mushrooms reduce in size and start to brown, 3 to 5 minutes. While the mushrooms are cooking, drain the sun-dried tomatoes, discarding the soaking liquid, and finely chop them. Add the kale and sun-dried tomatoes to the pan and cook for another couple of minutes, or until the kale turns bright green. Turn off the heat. If there is any excess liquid in the pan, drain it off and discard. Add the lemon juice and black pepper, and stir.

Now, it's time to assemble. Spread 1 cup (240 ml) of the marinara sauce on the bottom of a 9 x 13-inch (23 x 33-cm) casserole dish. Layer the lasagna noodles so they cover the bottom of the dish but are not overlapping. I like to break up pieces of an additional lasagna noodle to cover up any large gaps or spaces. Evenly spread 1¼ cups (300 g) of the ricotta over the noodles. Next, spread half of the mushroom and kale mixture over the ricotta. Pour 1 cup (240 ml) of marinara sauce over the veggies.

Arrange another layer of noodles over the marinara followed by 1¼ cups (300 g) of the ricotta, the other half of the veggies and 1 cup (240 ml) of the marinara. Arrange the final layer of noodles over the top and finish with 1½ cups (355 ml) of marinara. Drop equal-sized dollops of the remaining ricotta along the top of the lasagna and use the back of a spoon to gently spread them into circles.

Cover the dish tightly with tinfoil and bake for 40 minutes. Remove the tinfoil and continue to bake for another 10 to 15 minutes, or until the edges of the ricotta dollops begin to brown. Remove the lasagna from the oven and let rest, lightly covered, for 10 to 15 minutes. Using a sharp knife, cut the lasagna into nine pieces and serve.

NOTE

If you aren't gluten-free, use oven-ready whole wheat lasagna noodles.

SAUCY VERMICELLI WITH VEGETABLES AND FRESH HERBS

1½ cups (222 g) frozen shelled edamame

3 (1.8-oz [50-g]) nests (5.5-oz [150 g total]) brown rice vermicelli

ALMOND CITRUS SAUCE

⅓ cup (85 g) stirred almond butter

4 tsp (21 g) white miso

⅓ cup (80 ml) fresh orange juice

3 tbsp (45 ml) fresh lime juice

2 tbsp (30 ml) apple cider vinegar

2 tbsp (30 ml) tamari

1 tbsp (15 ml) pure maple syrup (optional)

2 cloves garlic, crushed and peeled

1 (¾″ [2-cm]) knob fresh ginger, peeled, or 2 tsp (4 g) grated

1½ tsp (8 ml) vinegar-based hot sauce (e.g., Frank's RedHot), or to your preference

¼ cup (60 ml) water

Thin, wiry vermicelli has become our last-minute dinner noodle, especially in the warmer months when we want a lighter meal but we're craving the comfort of carb-y noodles. They need only a quick soak to soften, and when tossed with this zesty almond butter citrus sauce, they're filling and moreish—I can't resist at least a small serving of seconds. Finely chopped and thinly sliced vegetables are the secret to pleasing veggie-packed meals, so be sure to prep the vegetables accordingly. I like to use a mandoline to slice the red cabbage as thinly as possible—the thinner, the better for this dish. Similarly, keep your broccoli florets small and cut into ¼- to ½-inch (0.6- to 1.3-cm) pieces. Note that, unlike many recipes where herbs are used as garnish, here they're a key ingredient—so don't skip them, and feel free to add more. If you aren't a cilantro lover, use more mint or replace it with fresh basil.

Bring a large pot of water to a boil. Once boiling, turn the heat down to low, add the edamame and simmer, uncovered, for 3 to 4 minutes. Remove the edamame with a slotted spoon and set them aside. Don't empty the pot; we'll use it again.

Now, plunge the vermicelli into the same pot of water. Let the noodles sit, fully submerged, in the hot water for 5 minutes (set a timer!). Meanwhile, fill a large bowl with ice-cold water. After 5 minutes, scoop out ½ cup (120 ml) of the cooking liquid from the pot and set it aside. Drain the noodles, give them a good rinse and place them in the bowl of ice water. This keeps the noodles from overcooking and sticking together.

While the vermicelli is soaking and cooling, make the almond citrus sauce: In a blender, combine the almond butter, miso, orange and lime juice, vinegar, tamari, maple syrup (if using), garlic, ginger, hot sauce and water, and blend until smooth. Set aside.

(continued)

3 cups (213 g) small broccoli florets (no bigger than ½″ [1.3 cm] wide)

1½ cups (180 g) matchstick-cut carrots

1 red bell pepper, seeded, stemmed and thinly sliced

1 cup (90 g) thinly sliced red cabbage

1 cup loosely packed (20 g) fresh cilantro leaves and tender stems, chopped

1 cup loosely packed (40 g) fresh mint leaves, chopped

¼ cup (36 g) chopped or sliced almonds

Now, heat a large sauté pan over medium heat. Add the broccoli, carrots, red pepper and a few tablespoons (about 30 ml) of water to the pan and cook, stirring, for 4 to 5 minutes, or until the broccoli is bright green and fork-tender and the veggies are heated throughout. Add water, if needed, to prevent burning.

Drain the noodles again and add them to the pan along with the edamame. Pour in the almond citrus sauce and toss everything together with tongs. Use a fork to tease the noodles apart if they are stuck together in clumps. Add some of the reserved hot cooking water if needed to loosen. Fold in the cabbage, cilantro and mint. Divide among bowls, top with chopped almonds and serve.

> NOTE
>
> *For a nut-free option, substitute sunflower seed butter for the almond butter and sunflower seeds for the almonds.*

EGGPLANT PUTTANESCA WITH WALNUTS

MAKES 3 TO 4 SERVINGS

¾ cup (75 g) walnuts

1 globe eggplant (1 to 1½ lb [455 to 680 g])

Sea salt

5 cloves garlic, minced

1 tsp dried oregano

¼ tsp red pepper flakes, or to your preference

3 (15-oz [425-g]) cans diced tomatoes

¼ cup (25 g) pitted black olives (packed in water), thinly sliced

¼ cup (25 g) pitted green olives (packed in water), thinly sliced

2 tbsp (17 g) capers, drained and roughly chopped

1 tbsp (4 g) nutritional yeast

Freshly ground black pepper

12 oz (340 g) dried fusilli pasta of choice (brown rice, chickpea, red lentil or quinoa)

There are evenings when I want big flavor without a lot of time committed to the kitchen. This walnutty spin on puttanesca is a recipe I turn to when I want something robust, spicy and savory. Quickly. And I'm always excited to have new ways to use the often misunderstood and underutilized eggplant. Because if you don't like eggplant, chances are you've had undercooked eggplant, which is spongy and bitter. When eggplant is cooked properly, it's creamy and delicious, and collapses easily under a fork. Any pasta shape or type will do, but I tend to pair a legume-based pasta with this chunky sauce.

Preheat the oven to 350°F (180°C) and line a baking sheet with parchment paper. Spread out the walnuts on the prepared pan and toast in the oven for 8 minutes, or until lightly browned and fragrant. Transfer them immediately to a plate to cool. Once cooled, place the walnuts in a food processor and process until fine and crumbly. Be careful not to overprocess or you'll end up with walnut butter. Set aside.

Peel the eggplant and cut it into 1-inch (2.5-cm) cubes.

Heat a large, nonstick pan over low to medium heat and add the eggplant plus a small pinch of salt. Cook for 10 minutes, stirring occasionally, until the eggplant is browned and begins to shrink. Here we're dry-frying the eggplant, but if it starts to stick, you can add a little bit of water as needed.

While the eggplant is cooking in the pan, bring a large pot of salted water to a boil.

Next, add the garlic, oregano and red pepper flakes to the eggplant pan. Add a little water and cook for another 30 seconds while stirring.

(continued)

Drain the canned tomatoes (reserve the liquid for your next soup or vegetable broth) and add them to the pan. Cover and cook over medium heat for 10 minutes. The tomatoes should start falling apart.

Add the olives and capers to the pan and cook, uncovered, stirring occasionally, for another 5 minutes, over low to medium heat. Stir in the walnuts, nutritional yeast and black pepper, and turn off the heat. The puttanesca will be thick. Cover until the pasta is done.

Meanwhile, once the water is boiling, cook the pasta according to the package directions for al dente. When done, reserve ½ cup (120 ml) of the pasta cooking water, then drain the pasta.

Add the drained pasta to the pan of veggies and toss to combine. Add ¼ cup (60 ml) of the reserved pasta water to loosen the pasta. Add more, if needed. Divide among bowls and serve immediately.

MAC 'N' CAULI CREAM

MAKES 4 TO 6 SERVINGS ❀ NUT-FREE OPTION

3 cups (300 g) bite-sized cauliflower florets

1 cup (150 g) chopped yellow onion

1 cup (130 g) chopped carrot

1 cup (140 g) raw cashews, soaked in hot water for 1 to 3 hours

¼ cup (16 g) nutritional yeast

1½ tsp (4.5 g) garlic powder

1 tsp onion powder

1 tsp sea salt

2 tsp (10 ml) Dijon mustard

Juice of ½ large lemon

1 cup (240 ml) unsweetened almond or organic soy milk

1 lb (455 g) dried brown rice or quinoa elbow macaroni

¾ cup (54 g) Italian Parmesan (see below) or your preferred vegan Parmesan

ITALIAN PARMESAN

1 cup (145 g) almonds, cashews or sunflower seeds

¼ cup (16 g) nutritional yeast

1 tsp sea salt, or to your preference

1½ tsp (3.5 g) Italian seasoning (see page 70 to make your own)

½ tsp garlic powder

Mac and cheese, *the* comfort food, is usually calorie dense and nutrient deficient, but not this one. This version has a supercreamy sauce made from vegetables, the highlight being cauliflower—a true superfood. The veggies are steamed and blended into the cashew-based cheese sauce, making the cauliflower more palatable to those who don't love it but want to eat it.

First, steam the vegetables: Fit a steamer basket into a medium-sized to large pot and fill with water to just below the basket. Bring to a boil. Once boiling place the cauliflower, onion and carrot in the basket and cover. Steam for 10 to 15 minutes, or until the veggies are very tender. Remove from the heat and set aside.

Bring a large pot of salted water to a boil.

Drain the cashews, discarding the soaking liquid, and place them in a high-speed blender along with the steamed veggies, nutritional yeast, garlic and onion powders, salt, Dijon mustard, lemon juice and milk. Blend on high speed until completely smooth. Set aside.

Add the pasta to the boiling water and cook according to the package directions for al dente.

While the pasta is cooking, make the Italian Parmesan: In a food processor, combine all its ingredients and process until a sand-like texture is reached. Transfer the Parmesan to a lidded jar (it will keep in the fridge for up to 3 months).

When the pasta is cooked, drain well (don't rinse) and return it back to the pot. Pour in the blended sauce and mix until creamy. Divide the pasta among bowls and top each bowl with 1 to 2 tablespoons (5 to 10 g) Italian Parmesan.

> NOTE
>
> *For a nut-free option, use sunflower seeds instead of cashews.*

ONE-POT TUSCAN PASTA

1 leek, dark green tips and root removed and discarded, halved lengthwise and thinly sliced

4 cloves garlic, minced

10 oz (280 g) portobello mushrooms, thinly sliced (4 portobellos)

1 tbsp (6 g) Italian seasoning (see Notes to make your own)

¼ tsp red pepper flakes (optional)

1 (15-oz [425-g]) can diced tomatoes

1 (15-oz [425-g]) can tomato sauce or passata

2¾ cups (650 ml) low-sodium vegetable stock

½ tsp sea salt, or to taste

10 oz (280 g) dried brown rice spaghetti or linguine

1½ cups (273 g) cooked or canned borlotti, navy or (384 g) cannellini beans, drained and rinsed

1 tsp coconut sugar (optional)

1½ cups packed (60 g) baby spinach (optional)

3 tbsp (12 g) nutritional yeast

1 tsp red wine vinegar

Freshly ground black pepper

OPTIONAL GARNISH

Fresh thyme or oregano

This pasta is guaranteed to please everyone at the table. The Italian-inspired tomato sauce, mushrooms and pasta are cooked together simultaneously and served hot right from the pot. I've used portobello mushrooms for their extra-meaty texture, but you can use any variety you love. The coconut sugar balances the acidity of the tomatoes but is optional, as is the addition of red pepper flakes and spinach.

In a Dutch oven or soup pot, sauté the leeks and garlic with a few tablespoons (about 30 ml) of water over medium heat for 5 minutes or until softened. Add water, as needed, to prevent burning.

Add the mushrooms, Italian seasoning and red pepper flakes, and continue to sauté for another 5 minutes, or until the mushrooms have shrunken in size and begin releasing their juices. Now, add the diced tomatoes, tomato sauce, vegetable stock and salt, and bring to a boil. Crack the pasta in half and add to the pot along with the beans. Lower the heat to a rapid simmer and simmer, uncovered, for 12 to 15 minutes, or until the pasta is tender and the sauce has thickened. Stir often to prevent the noodles from sticking together or to the bottom of the pot and make sure the noodles are always submerged in the sauce. Toward the end of the cooking time and as the sauce thickens, it might start sputtering and splashing. If so, partially cover the pot to avoid a mess.

Turn off the heat. Stir in the coconut sugar (if using), spinach (if using), nutritional yeast and vinegar. Taste and reseason with pepper and salt, as needed, and divide among bowls. Garnish with fresh thyme, if desired.

> ### NOTES
>
> *If you don't have leeks, use one large yellow onion, diced.*
>
> *If you eat gluten, you can use an equal amount of whole wheat spaghetti or linguine.*
>
> *To make your own Italian seasoning, mix together:*
>
> *1 teaspoon dried basil, ¾ teaspoon dried oregano, ¾ teaspoon dried parsley and ½ teaspoon dried rosemary.*

MUHAMARRA PASTA

MAKES 4 SERVINGS

SAUCE

3 large red bell peppers (600 g), or 1 cup packed (180 g) roasted peppers

¾ cup (75 g) walnuts

1¼ tsp (2.5 g) ground cumin

¼ to ½ tsp red pepper flakes, or to your preference

Juice of ½ lemon

1 tbsp (15 ml) balsamic vinegar

1 large clove garlic, crushed and peeled

¼ tsp sea salt, or to taste

Freshly ground black pepper

1 rounded tbsp (9 g) drained capers, plus more for garnish

PASTA

12 oz (340 g) dried fusilli pasta (brown rice, chickpea or red lentil)

Muhammara is a Middle Eastern dip made of roasted red peppers and toasted walnuts. I've flipped this delicious dip into a simple and incredibly flavorful pasta. The traditional version includes bread crumbs and pomegranate molasses; I've skipped both and instead have made it loose, like a sauce, and a touch more savory by adding capers. I reach for a spiraled pasta when making this recipe, as the textured sauce coats and catches in the curves and swirls. Adjust the red pepper flakes to your liking or omit if you don't like any heat.

Roast the peppers: To roast your peppers, if not using jarred, preheat the oven to 450°F (230°C). Line a large baking sheet with parchment paper. Place the whole peppers on the prepared baking sheet and roast in the oven for 45 to 60 minutes, rotating every 15 to 20 minutes until all sides are charred. Remove the peppers from the oven and place in a heatproof bowl. Lower the temperature to 350°F (180°C) or turn off if continuing with the recipe later. Cover the bowl with a plate and let the peppers steam for 20 to 30 minutes—this helps loosen their skins. Once cool enough to handle, peel the peppers and remove and discard the stem, core and seeds. Your peppers are now ready.

Line the baking sheet with a fresh piece of parchment paper. Spread out the walnuts on the pan and toast in the oven (preheated to 350°F [180°C]) for 8 minutes, or until golden and fragrant, keeping a close eye on them for the last 2 minutes to prevent burning. Remove them from the oven and transfer to a plate to cool for 5 minutes. Meanwhile, bring a large pot of salted water to a boil.

Make the sauce: In a food processor, combine the roasted peppers, toasted walnuts, cumin, red pepper flakes, lemon juice, vinegar, garlic, salt, black pepper and capers, and process until almost smooth but not quite. Set aside.

Make the pasta: Once the water is boiling, cook the pasta according to the package directions for al dente. Reserve ½ cup (120 ml) of pasta water, then drain the pasta and transfer it back to the pot. Add the muhamarra sauce and toss everything together. Add some reserved pasta water, as needed, to thin. Spoon into bowls and garnish with extra capers.

PAD THAI–INSPIRED NOODLES WITH TEMPEH AND BROCCOLI

MAKES 3 SERVINGS 🌱 NUT-FREE OPTION

1 (8-oz [225-g]) package tempeh

¼ cup (60 ml) fresh lime juice (from 2 to 3 limes)

¼ cup (60 ml) low-sodium tamari

1 tbsp + 2 tsp (25 g) tamarind paste

1 tbsp (5 g) peeled and finely grated ginger

1½ tsp (8 ml) vinegar-based hot sauce (e.g., Frank's RedHot)

¼ cup (64 g) stirred almond or all-natural peanut butter

1 red or yellow bell pepper, seeded, stemmed and thinly sliced

8 oz (225 g) dried brown rice fettuccine, spaghetti or linguine

4 cups (360 g) bite-sized broccoli florets

2 green onions, thinly sliced

1 large bunch cilantro, tender stems and leaves only

Lime wedges, for serving

NOTE

For a nut-free version, use sunflower seed butter or tahini instead of nut butter.

This tasty combination borrows a lot from pad thai—lime, tamarind and tamari—but is creamier, thanks to nut butter that's stirred right into the hot noodles before serving. Add protein-rich, marinated tempeh and nutritious broccoli and you've whipped up a well-rounded bowl. This recipe moves fast once the noodles are cooked, so it's helpful to prep all your veggies ahead of time.

Break the tempeh into a few pieces and place it in a food processor. Pulse until crumbly. Alternatively, you can finely chop the tempeh.

In a medium-sized bowl or glass container, whisk together the lime juice, tamari, tamarind, ginger and hot sauce. Place the tempeh in the container or bowl and mix well. Cover and refrigerate for anywhere from 20 minutes to 1 hour.

Bring a large pot of salted water to a boil. Place the nut butter in a medium-sized heatproof bowl and set it aside.

While waiting for the water to boil, heat a large pan (nonstick works well here) over medium heat. Add the marinated tempeh and any leftover marinade and cook for 3 to 4 minutes, stirring. Add water, 1 tablespoon (15 ml) at a time, to prevent sticking. Next, add the bell pepper and cook for another few minutes, stirring often, until the peppers are just tender. Turn off the heat.

Once the water is boiling, cook the pasta according to the package directions for al dente; when 3 minutes are left to go on the pasta, add the broccoli to the pot as well. Reserve 1 cup (240 ml) of the pasta cooking water, then drain the pasta and broccoli in a colander.

Transfer the drained pasta and broccoli to the pan that contains the tempeh and peppers. Add about ⅓ cup (80 ml) of the hot pasta water and toss to loosen. Add another ¼ cup (60 ml) of the pasta water to the bowl of nut butter and whisk until smooth, then pour into the pan. Toss everything together, using tongs. Add more pasta water, if needed, to loosen.

Divide the pasta among three bowls and generously garnish each bowl with green onions, cilantro and a lime wedge. Serve immediately.

ALFREDO AND ROASTED SPROUTS

MAKES 3 TO 4 SERVINGS

This is a whole food take on a classic sauce made from what I consider to be the most practical plant-based food group: beans. This iteration of Alfredo is pleasantly unconventional and has been in my rotation for years. The sauce is made by blending nuts and navy beans and then tossing it with hot pasta and roasted Brussels sprouts. I like to steam the sprouts for a few minutes before popping them into the oven, so they're tender throughout without burning on the edges. If Brussels sprouts aren't your favorite, roast some broccoli or cauliflower, or add a couple of handfuls of spinach to the cooking pasta instead.

PASTA AND SPROUTS

5 cups (450 g) Brussels sprouts

2 tbsp (30 ml) aquafaba, or 1 tbsp (15 ml) fresh lemon juice

Sea salt and freshly ground black pepper

12 to 16 oz (340 to 455 g) dried brown rice or quinoa linguine

ALFREDO SAUCE

¼ cup (36 g) raw almonds, soaked in water for 6 to 8 hours, or ¼ cup (35 g) raw cashews, soaked in hot water for 1 to 3 hours

¾ cup (175 ml) unsweetened almond or organic soy milk, plus more as needed

1½ cups (273 g) cooked or canned navy beans, drained and rinsed

2 tbsp (8 g) nutritional yeast

1 tbsp (16 g) white miso

Juice of ½ large lemon

2 tsp (10 g) Dijon mustard

1 tsp garlic powder

¾ tsp onion powder

⅛ tsp ground nutmeg

Pinch of red pepper flakes

Pinch of freshly ground black pepper, or more to taste

FOR GARNISH

Italian Parmesan (page 69; optional)

Chopped fresh parsley (optional)

First make the sprouts: Preheat the oven to 425°F (220°C) and line a baking sheet with parchment paper.

Trim the Brussels sprouts, cutting any large ones in half. Fit a steamer basket into a medium-sized pot and fill the pot with water to just below the basket, then cover and bring to a boil. Once boiling, place the sprouts in the basket, cover and steam until not quite fork-tender and bright green, about 5 minutes. Transfer the sprouts to the prepared baking sheet. Toss them with the aquafaba and sprinkle with a pinch of salt and black pepper. Roast them in the oven for 15 to 20 minutes, or until fork-tender and beginning to brown on the edges.

Meanwhile, bring a large pot of salted water to a boil. Cook the pasta according to the package directions for al dente.

While the pasta is cooking, make the Alfredo sauce: Drain the nuts, discarding the soaking liquid, and place them in a high-speed blender along with the milk, beans, nutritional yeast, miso, lemon juice, Dijon mustard, garlic and onion powders, nutmeg, red pepper flakes and black pepper. Blend on high speed until the sauce is completely smooth. Add more milk, 1 tablespoon (15 ml) at a time, if needed to thin the sauce so it's pourable but still thick.

Once the pasta is cooked, reserve ½ cup (120 ml) of the cooking liquid, then drain the pasta in a colander. Return the pasta to the pot. Add the Alfredo sauce and sprouts, and toss to combine. If the pasta is too thick, add some reserved cooking liquid and toss again. Taste and reseason with salt and black pepper, if needed. Divide among bowls and garnish with Italian Parmesan and/or parsley.

FORGET THE FORK: HANDHELD MAINS

There's something undeniably satisfying about getting your hands involved, right? Eliminating the cutlery seems to elevate the experience by making the simple act of eating more intimate and exciting. It's just better! Dripping sauces, messy hands, strategic bites—it's no wonder so many classic comfort foods are handheld. These recipes are all about combining fun and flavor with nutrition, which isn't very difficult. It just takes some creativity and maybe a little planning.

This chapter gets used a lot in my kitchen, so make notes and earmark your favorites. I keep a stock of Walnut and Black Bean Burgers (page 84) in the freezer for burger night and the speedy Avocado Edamame Smash Wraps (page 93) have been served for any and every meal, depending on the day! This chapter is particularly popular on the weekends when we're in the mood for something tasty with a takeout or order-in vibe.

THIN-CRUST PIZZA WITH ROASTED BUTTERNUT SQUASH AND ARUGULA

MAKES 1 (9½-INCH [24-CM]) PIZZA

TOPPINGS

3 cups (450 g) peeled and cubed butternut squash (¾-inch [2-cm] chunks)

1 large yellow onion, cut into 1″ (2.5-cm) pieces

Sea salt and freshly ground black pepper

¾ cup (180 g) White Bean Hummus (recipe follows) or preferred hummus

2 large handfuls of baby arugula

A good pizza crust recipe is essential, especially if you follow a gluten-free diet. I've made this crust over and over and it fits the bill—I share it with pride! It's crispy and light and multipurpose (it's also the potpie pastry for the Moroccan Potpies on page 141). The rolling pin is required but preparation and assembly are low maintenance. I'm obsessed with the trio of sweet butternut squash, peppery arugula and garlicky hummus, but you can play with your favorite pizza toppings. I've also included my preferred pizza hummus, but you can use any that you love. Bernard and I will split this pizza and pair it with a green salad for dinner, but it can easily be enjoyed solo, or even shared with four as an appetizer.

Position the oven rack in the middle of the oven and preheat to 400°F (200°C). Line a large baking sheet or pizza pan with parchment paper.

Start the toppings: Spread out the butternut squash and onion on the prepared pan, making sure to not overcrowd the pan. Season with salt and black pepper and bake for 30 minutes. The onion should be browned, and the squash tender and beginning to brown on the edges. Remove from the oven and set the vegetables and parchment paper aside. We'll use the pan again. Lower the oven temperature to 375°F (190°C).

(continued)

PIZZA CRUST

1½ tsp (3 g) whole psyllium husk

¼ cup (60 ml) water

1 cup (96 g) blanched almond flour

½ cup (80 g) brown rice flour

2 tbsp (8 g) nutritional yeast

1 tsp garlic powder

¼ tsp red pepper flakes (optional)

½ tsp sea salt

1 tbsp (15 ml) apple cider vinegar

While the veggies are roasting, prepare the pizza crust: In a small bowl, combine the psyllium husk and water. Stir and let sit for 5 minutes to thicken.

While the mixture thickens, in a medium-sized bowl, stir together the almond flour, brown rice flour, nutritional yeast, garlic powder, red pepper flakes (if using), salt and vinegar. Add the thickened psyllium mixture and mix with a nonstick spatula until combined. It will be a little crumbly, but it will come together once kneaded. Be sure to wipe the spatula and get any stuck-on bits into the bowl; every bit of moisture counts. Then, with clean hands, knead the mixture together briefly until a doughlike consistency is reached. Add 1 to 3 teaspoons (5 to 15 ml) of water if the dough is dry or crumbles. Shape it into a tight ball and let it rest for a few minutes.

Prepare two pieces of parchment paper, each about 10 inches (25.5 cm) long.

Place the dough on the middle of one piece of the parchment and place the other piece of parchment on top. Using a rolling pin, roll out the dough evenly into a 9½-inch (24.5-cm) circle, keeping the dough about ¼ inch (6 mm) thick. The dough will splay and crack along the edges as it's rolled; this is normal. I like to lay a 9- to 10-inch (23- to 25.5-cm) round baking pan or bowl on top of the dough and cut around the edges. Feel around for any thin spots and work the cut-off pieces into the dough and roll again. Repeat until you have a nice shape. It doesn't need to be perfect.

Peel the dough gently off the parchment and flip it onto its other side (this keeps the dough from sticking to the parchment), then place on the baking sheet. Bake for 20 minutes, or until the whole dough lifts when you pick up the edge.

Remove the pizza from the oven and spread the hummus evenly over the dough. Distribute the squash and onion over the top. Bake again for another 12 to 15 minutes, or until the edges of the crust are starting to brown. Remove the pizza from the oven, scatter the arugula on top and sprinkle with red pepper flakes for extra spice, if desired. Cut into slices and serve immediately.

WHITE BEAN HUMMUS

MAKES 1⅓ CUPS (320 G)

1½ cups (273 g) cooked or canned navy beans, drained and rinsed

2 cloves garlic, crushed and peeled

2 tablespoons (30 ml) fresh lemon juice

2 tablespoons (30 g) stirred tahini or (32 g) cashew butter

¼ teaspoon sea salt, or to taste

3 tablespoons (45 ml) aquafaba or water, or more as needed

This is a multipurpose bean spread that you can also use as a vegetable dip, on sandwiches, or even stirred into hot pasta! It's creamy with a little extra hint of garlic. I love navy beans for their mild taste. They're also also a convenient source of iron.

In a food processor, combine the beans, garlic, lemon juice, tahini, salt and aquafaba, and process continuously for a few minutes, until smooth. Add more aquafaba, as needed, to thin. You want the hummus to be thick and creamy.

83

WALNUT AND BLACK BEAN BURGERS WITH SPECIAL SAUCE

MAKES 5 BURGERS

BURGERS

2 tbsp (14 g) ground flaxseeds

3 tbsp (45 ml) water

1 cup (100 g) walnuts

1 cup (150 g) diced yellow onion

4 large cloves garlic, minced

¾ cup (75 g) gluten-free oat flour

2 tbsp (8 g) nutritional yeast

2 tsp (4 g) dried basil

1 tsp ground cumin

Pinch of freshly ground black pepper

½ tsp sea salt

1½ cups (258 g) cooked or canned black beans, drained and rinsed

2 tbsp (30 ml) tamari

1 tbsp (15 ml) Dijon mustard

FOR SERVING

Preferred whole-grain buns or sturdy lettuce leaves

Lettuce

Sliced tomatoes

Sliced onions

Pickles

Every time I make these burgers, I talk myself out of having seconds. I'm satisfied after one (they're filling!) but I want more of that flavor! They've quickly become one of our favorite whole food burgers. They offer protein, fiber, omega-3 fatty acids, fiber, iron—so much good stuff. You can top them how you like but the Special Sauce is beyond delicious . . . addictive, even.

Make the burgers: Preheat the oven to 375°F (190°C). Line a large baking sheet with parchment paper. In a small bowl, mix the ground flaxseeds with the water and set aside for 5 minutes to thicken.

In a food processor, process the walnuts until fine and crumbly, then transfer to a large bowl.

In a medium-sized pan, sauté the onion with a few tablespoons (about 30 ml) of water until the onion is translucent and soft, 7 to 10 minutes. Add water, as needed, to prevent burning. Add the garlic and cook for another 30 seconds. Remove from the heat, drain and discard any excess water, then transfer the onion and garlic to the food processor.

Place the remaining burger ingredients, oat flour through Dijon mustard, in the food processor along with the thickened flax mixture. Process continuously until everything is combined and the beans are no longer whole.

(continued)

SPECIAL SAUCE

¾ cup (105 g) raw cashews, soaked for 1 to 3 hours in hot water, or 1 (12-oz [340-g]) package extra-firm silken tofu

1 tbsp (15 ml) yellow mustard

1½ tsp (8 ml) vinegar-based hot sauce (e.g., Frank's RedHot)

2 tsp (10 ml) apple cider vinegar

2 tsp (10 ml) pure maple syrup

1 tsp garlic powder

1 tsp onion powder

¼ tsp sea salt

½ cup (120 ml) water (omit if using silken tofu), plus more if needed

2 tsp (2 g) dried dill

Transfer the mixture to the bowl of walnuts. Mix with a spatula or large spoon until well incorporated and no dry spots remain. The mixture will be thick and sticky. Using a ½-cup (120-ml) measuring cup, scoop out a level ½ cup and form into 3-inch (7.5-cm)-wide, 1 inch (2.5-cm)-thick patties and place at least 2 inches apart on the prepared baking sheet. Having slightly damp hands and rinsing your hands after shaping a couple of burgers will reduce the stickiness.

Bake for 30 minutes, then, using a thin spatula, gently flip and bake for another 5 to 10 minutes. They're done when the edges are browned and they're no longer soft in the middle. Let the burgers rest for 10 to 15 minutes before serving; they firm up as they cool.

While the burgers are in the oven, make the special sauce: If using cashews, drain them, discarding the soaking liquid, and place them in a blender along with the remaining sauce ingredients, except the dill. Blend until completely smooth. Now, add the dill and blend briefly to combine. If using silken tofu, follow the same procedure but omit the water.

Serve the burger on your preferred whole-grain bun or in large sturdy lettuce leaves. Top with special sauce and your favorite burger fixings.

The sauce will keep in the fridge for 3 to 5 days.

SLOPPY LENTIL PORTOBELLOS WITH HERB AND KALE PESTO

MAKES 8 SLOPPY PORTOBELLO MUSHROOMS

SLOPPY PORTOBELLOS

8 (4″ [10-cm]) portobello mushrooms

1 yellow onion, diced

1 red bell pepper, seeded, stemmed and diced

3 large cloves garlic, minced

1½ tsp (4 g) smoked paprika

1½ tsp (4 g) chili powder

1 tsp ground cumin

½ tsp dried oregano

2 tbsp (30 ml) tamari

2 tbsp (18 g) coconut sugar or (40 g) molasses

1¾ cups (15-oz [425-g]) passata or tomato sauce

1 cup (190 g) dried split red lentils

2 cups (475 ml) low-sodium vegetable stock

The bun situation on a gluten-free diet can be challenging, or sometimes irritating, so I wanted to do a sloppy joe makeover that didn't require one. Cue portobellos! This mature riff on a traditional homestyle meal is smoky, savory, a little sweet and a little sloppy even without the bun! However, if you have some, feel free to go big with this recipe and layer the mushrooms, lentil filling and herb pesto inside your favorite whole-grain bun or even bread. Napkins will most definitely be required. The herbed pesto is a perfect match for the tangy lentil filling but if you're short on time or would rather have a simpler option, you can use avocado or vegan sour cream instead.

Start with the portobellos: Line a large baking pan with parchment paper. Wipe the mushrooms clean. Remove and finely chop the stems and set them aside. Place the mushroom caps upside down (gill side up) on the prepared pan. Set aside.

In a medium-sized pot, sauté the onion and bell pepper with ¼ cup (60 ml) water, stirring often, for 10 minutes, or until softened. Add more water, as needed, to prevent burning.

Add the diced mushroom stems, garlic, smoked paprika, chili powder, cumin, oregano, tamari and coconut sugar, and cook for 2 to 3 minutes.

Now, add the passata, lentils and stock, and bring to a simmer. Simmer, uncovered, stirring often to prevent sticking, for 15 to 20 minutes, or until the lentils are just tender and the mixture is thick and chunky. Turn off the heat.

Now preheat the oven to 375°F (190°C). Place the mushroom caps in the oven and bake for 15 to 17 minutes. Pour off any liquid that has pooled in the mushroom or sop up the liquid with napkins.

(continued)

1½ cups (150 g) walnuts

Sea salt and freshly ground black pepper

HERB AND KALE PESTO

1 cup (67 g) roughly chopped curly or lacinato kale

1 cup (20 g) fresh cilantro leaves and tender stems

1 cup (40 g) fresh basil leaves

1 cup (40 g) fresh mint leaves

½ avocado, peeled and pitted

1 large clove garlic, crushed and peeled

Juice of ½ large lemon

½ sea salt, or to taste

¼ cup (60 ml) water, plus more if needed

Meanwhile, in a food processor, pulse the walnuts until fine and crumbly. Remove ½ cup (50 g) of walnuts from the processor and stir them into the lentil mixture (keep the rest of the walnuts in the processor). Taste and season the lentils with salt and pepper, as needed. Cover to keep warm; the mixture will continue to thicken as it rests.

While the lentil mixture rests and the mushrooms are in the oven, make the pesto: Add the kale, cilantro, basil, mint, avocado, garlic, lemon juice, salt and water to the remaining pulsed walnuts in the food processor, and process continuously until creamy and no whole leaves are visible, adding more water if necessary.

Spoon about ½ cup (120 ml) of the lentil mixture onto each mushroom, followed by a generous dollop of pesto and serve.

SPICY SHEET PAN CAULIFLOWER TACOS

MAKES 8 TACOS NUT-FREE OPTION

SPICE BLEND

2 tbsp (8 g) nutritional yeast

1 tbsp (8 g) chili powder

1 tsp ground cumin

1 tsp onion powder

1 tsp garlic powder

1 tsp sweet paprika

Pinch of freshly ground black pepper

CAULIFLOWER AND BLACK BEAN FILLING

1 medium-sized head cauliflower, cut into 1″ (2.5-cm) florets (about 5 cups [500 g])

1½ cups (258 g) cooked or canned black beans or chickpeas, drained and rinsed

¼ cup (60 ml) vinegar-based hot sauce (e.g., Frank's RedHot)

TO SERVE

8 (5″ [12.5-cm]) corn tortillas, or sturdy lettuce leaves

1 head leafy green lettuce, chopped, or ¼ head purple or green cabbage, shredded

2 cups (520 g) salsa of choice

1 red onion, finely diced

2 tomatoes, diced

2 avocados, pitted and peeled, sliced or diced

Cashew Sour Cream (page 120; optional)

3 limes, sliced into wedges

Growing up a taco night meant one thing—the same taco we had every other taco night. Today, we approach tacos much, much differently—anything and everything goes, from the elaborate and epicurean to the plain and humble! And I've never met a taco I didn't love. These tacos are sheet pan–easy while still having all the flavor, texture and messiness required from a tasty taco. The cauliflower and beans are tossed in hot sauce and spices and then baked. After spooning the filling into tortillas, layer them generously with all the toppings—it's all about the toppings! A squeeze of lime and dollop of salsa onto each taco is essential as the filling, once out of the oven, is more dry than juicy.

Preheat the oven to 400°F (200°C) and line a baking sheet with parchment paper.

Make the spice blend: In a small bowl, combine the nutritional yeast, chili powder, cumin, onion and garlic powders, paprika and pepper, and set aside.

Make the filling: In a large bowl, combine the cauliflower florets and beans. Drizzle the hot sauce over the top and toss to coat everything evenly. Now, spread half of the spice blend over the top and mix again. Then, add the rest of the spice blend and mix again until all the cauliflower and beans are coated.

Transfer to the prepared baking sheet and bake for 20 minutes. Flip and redistribute in a single layer, then bake for another 10 to 15 minutes, or until the cauliflower is fork-tender and might be beginning to char on the edges.

Meanwhile, warm the corn tortillas in the oven or in a large sauté pan over medium heat.

Layer each tortilla with lettuce, salsa, spicy cauliflower and black bean filling, onion, tomato, avocado, Cashew Sour Cream (if using) and a generous squeeze of lime juice.

AVOCADO EDAMAME SMASH WRAPS

MAKES 3 TO 4 WRAPS 🌱 NUT-FREE

2 cups (296 g) frozen shelled edamame

2 avocados, pitted and peeled

2 cloves garlic, minced

2 tbsp (30 ml) fresh lemon juice, plus more as needed

½ tsp sea salt, plus more as needed

½ cup (70 g) finely chopped cucumber

3 cups (135 g) baby greens of choice

½ red onion, thinly sliced

Wraps of choice (brown rice, sprouted, raw coconut or flax)

A ripe avocado makes an easy meal. When I have one or two lying around, I know our next meal will be avo-centric and fuss-free. The chunky yet buttery avocado edamame mash is just delightful. It's a simple but unique duo that will make you want to pull up a chair and enjoy every bite. If you want to skip the wrap, you can also spoon this filling into sturdy lettuce leaves or baked potatoes, or on top of warm cooked grains.

Place the frozen edamame in a medium-sized pot and cover with an inch (2.5 cm) of water. Bring to a boil. Turn the heat down to low and simmer for 3 to 4 minutes. Drain the edamame and set them aside.

In a medium-sized bowl, mash the avocado. Add the garlic, lemon juice and salt.

Stir in the still-warm edamame. Mash some of the edamame and leave others whole. Fold in the cucumber, then taste and reseason with salt or lemon juice if needed.

Layer the greens, avocado edamame mash and red onion in each wrap. Roll up and serve.

> NOTE
>
> *If you eat gluten, you can use whole wheat or sprouted wraps.*

COZY CASSEROLES
AND SKILLETS

When there's something slowly cooking in the oven or simmering on the stove, the whole house feels warmer, more lived-in. A creamy casserole or a saucy skillet is incredibly inviting and is a sound remedy to a long day or brisk evening and, of course, the answer to feeding many mouths around the table. This kind of dinner can sometimes require a bit more effort or preparation, but the payoff is worth it.

I've included a variety in this chapter—some a little formal, such as the Modern Lentil Moussaka (page 101) others more casual, like the Queso Cruciferous Casserole (page 107)—but there's something for every occasion. These are also my favorite recipes to create and test because this is how I love to eat—mixtures and warm layered dishes with lots of veggies.

CHILI SHEPHERD'S PIE WITH SOUR CREAM POTATOES

MAKES 6 TO 9 SERVINGS

My Best Chili (page 119)

2¼ lb (1 kg) russet potatoes, peeled and cut into 1" (2.5-cm) chunks

1 cup (140 g) raw cashews, soaked in hot water for 1 to 3 hours

1½ tsp (8 g) Dijon mustard

1 tsp white miso

Juice of ½ lemon

1 tsp onion powder

½ tsp sea salt, or to taste

Scant 1 cup (230 ml) unsweetened soy milk

OPTIONAL GARNISHES

Thinly sliced chives or green onion

Parsley

NOTE

Try substituting sweet potatoes for white potatoes or using a mixture of both. I really like soy milk in these potatoes—it makes them super creamy—but you can also use oat or almond milk.

The best casserole dishes are often a combination of two or more layers. This cozy casserole pairs two comfort food heavy hitters: chili and creamy mashed potatoes. Delicious on top of delicious. This is a great dish to bring to a potluck, and if I watched sports or attended any big "game day" events, I think this would be my contribution! It's decidedly a crowd-pleaser. I prefer to make the chili the day before, to let the flavors develop and deepen overnight. This way, the cooking time is also shortened on the day I plan to serve it. It's especially important that the chili is simmered until thick for this casserole. Feel free to add a dash of hot sauce once plated!

First, make the chili (see page 119) or gently reheat the chili if made ahead of time.

Place the chopped potatoes in a large pot of salted water and bring to a boil. Once boiling, turn the heat down to low and simmer for 15 minutes, or until the potatoes are very tender.

While the potatoes are simmering, preheat the oven to 425°F (220°C). Drain the cashews, discarding the soaking liquid, and place them in a high-speed blender with the Dijon mustard, miso, lemon juice, onion powder, salt and milk. Blend on high speed until completely smooth. The consistency should be thick but pourable. Taste and reseason with salt, if needed. Set aside.

Once the potatoes are done, drain them well in a colander and return to the pot. Roughly mash the potatoes, then pour in the cashew mixture and mash and stir until creamy with no lumps. Taste and reseason with salt, if needed.

Transfer the warmed chili to a 9 x 13-inch (23 x 33-cm) casserole dish. Spread the mashed potatoes evenly over the top and slide the casserole dish into the oven. Bake for 15 minutes, or until the potato layer is golden. You can even turn on the broiler for a few minutes to get some extra color on the potato peaks. Remove the pie from the oven and let it rest for 5 minutes before serving. Feel free to garnish with chives or parsley.

97

MEDITERRANEAN CAULIFLOWER CASSEROLE

MAKES 4 SERVINGS · NUT-FREE

CASSEROLE

4 cups (400 g) bite-sized cauliflower florets

1 large red onion, thinly sliced

1 red or yellow bell pepper, cut into 1″ [2.5-cm] pieces

1 cup (100 g) pitted black or green olives, sliced if desired

1½ cups (255 g) cooked or canned chickpeas, drained and rinsed

1 cup (180 g) uncooked millet or white quinoa

1 cup (30 g) baby spinach

TAHINI SAUCE

⅓ cup (80 g) stirred tahini

⅓ cup (80 ml) fresh lemon juice

3 large cloves garlic, crushed and peeled

1 tbsp (15 ml) red wine vinegar

1½ tsp (2 g) dried oregano

1 tsp dried parsley

¾ cup (175 ml) water

1 tbsp (9 g) arrowroot starch

¼ tsp sea salt, or to taste

Pinch of black pepper

OPTIONAL GARNISHES

1 small bunch fresh mint

2 tbsp (16 g) sesame seeds

Lemon wedges

Getting a hot and wholesome meal on the table can be a challenge, but there are tips and tricks that make it easier. Filling a casserole dish and shoving it into the oven while you tend to other things is an approach I rely on. Fewer dishes are always a good thing, too. This casserole is built on fresh veggies that are chopped and glazed in a blitzed tahini sauce. It delivers in the nutrition department with cruciferous cauliflower and protein-rich chickpeas while singing the bright Mediterranean flavors of lemon, oregano and olives.

Preheat the oven to 450°F (230°C).

Start with the casserole: Put the cauliflower, onion, bell pepper, olives and chickpeas in a 9 x 13-inch (23 x 33-cm) casserole dish.

Make the tahini sauce: In a blender, combine the tahini, lemon juice, garlic, vinegar, oregano, parsley, water, arrowroot, salt and pepper, and blend until smooth. Pour the sauce over the vegetables in the casserole. Stir to coat all the veggies, then cover tightly with tinfoil.

Roast in the oven for 60 minutes, stirring once around the 40-minute mark. It's done when the cauliflower is fork-tender and the sauce is bubbling.

When there is about 20 minutes left on the casserole, cook the millet according to the package directions. Once cooked, fluff with a fork and cover until needed.

When the casserole is ready, remove it from the oven and stir in the spinach. Cover again for a few minutes to let the spinach wilt. Taste and reseason with salt, if needed.

Spoon the grains into bowls and top with the casserole. Garnish with mint and sesame seeds and serve with a lemon wedge.

MODERN LENTIL MOUSSAKA

MAKES 8 SERVINGS

2 lb (905 g) globe eggplant (2 to 3 eggplants)

½ tsp sea salt

Moussaka, a traditional Greek casserole, was my first encounter with eggplant. It was spectacular and I needed to make my own. In this plant-based version, prebaked eggplant slices are layered with a smoky lentil and tomato filling and finished with a velvety cashew béchamel. This is a clever casserole that's constructed like a lasagna, except eggplant replaces the pasta. A little extra effort is required to prep the eggplant, but it's time well spent. Sometimes, I like to pair it with a salad or cooked grains. Keeping the eggplant slices thin and uniform in size guarantees even cooking and a tender texture.

Preheat the oven to 425°F (220°C) and line two large baking sheets with parchment paper.

Slice the eggplants into ⅓-inch (0.75-cm) rounds (no thicker). Spread them out in a single layer on clean dish towels and sprinkle them evenly with salt (½ teaspoon in total). Let the eggplant rest for 30 minutes. Yes, it will seem like your kitchen is covered in eggplant, but just briefly. The salt will draw the moisture out of the eggplants, and they'll be covered with little water droplets.

After 30 minutes, blot or wipe away the moisture with another clean dish towel. Transfer the eggplant to the prepared baking sheets in a single layer and bake for 25 minutes, rotating the pans halfway through. The eggplants should be flexible and just tender. If you have thicker eggplant rounds, the cooking time will need to be extended. Remove the pans from the oven and set them aside. Lower the oven temperature to 375°F (190°C).

(continued)

MODERN LENTIL MOUSSAKA (CONTINUED)

LENTIL FILLING

1 large red onion, diced (2 cups [300 g])

6 cloves garlic, minced

1 tbsp (15 ml) tomato paste

2 tsp (2 g) dried oregano

1 tsp dried parsley

1 tsp sweet paprika

½ tsp ground cinnamon

¼ tsp red pepper flakes

¼ tsp freshly ground black pepper

8 oz (225 g) button or cremini mushrooms, diced

3 cups (594 g) cooked or canned brown or green lentils, drained and rinsed

1 (15-oz [425-g]) can tomato sauce or passata

1 (15-oz [425-g]) can diced tomatoes

½ tsp sea salt

1 tbsp (15 ml) red wine vinegar

CASHEW BÉCHAMEL

1½ cups (210 g) raw cashews, soaked in hot water for 1 to 3 hours

Scant ½ tsp ground nutmeg

¼ cup (60 ml) fresh lemon juice

2 cloves garlic, crushed and peeled

¾ tsp sea salt

Big pinch of freshly ground black pepper

¾ cup (175 ml) water

Meanwhile, start the filling: In a large sauté pan, sauté the onion with about ¼ cup (60 ml) water for 7 to 10 minutes, or until soft and translucent. Add water, as needed, to prevent burning.

Add the garlic, tomato paste, oregano, parsley, paprika, cinnamon, red pepper flakes, black pepper and mushrooms. Cook over medium heat, stirring often, for another 3 to 5 minutes, or until the mushrooms shrink and begin releasing their juices.

Add the lentils, tomato sauce, diced tomatoes, salt and vinegar and bring to a simmer. Simmer, uncovered, stirring occasionally, over low heat for 20 minutes, or until the mixture is thick. When you pull the lentils to the side, very little, if any, liquid should pool in the pan.

While the filling simmers, make the béchamel: Drain the cashews, discarding the soaking liquid, and place them in a high-speed blender along with the nutmeg, lemon juice, garlic, salt, pepper and water. Blend on high speed until completely smooth.

Spread half of the baked eggplant along the bottom of a 9 x 13-inch (23 x 33-cm) casserole dish (or similar size). Spoon all the lentil filling over the eggplants and spread it evenly. Top with the remaining eggplant slices, being careful to only overlap them slightly, and finally, pour the béchamel over the eggplant, smoothing it out into an even layer. You can add any leftover eggplant slices to your next sandwich, burger, or chop them and add to a stir-fry or soup.

Bake the moussaka, uncovered, for 30 to 35 minutes. The top will be golden and the edges will be just starting to brown. Remove the moussaka from the oven and let it rest for 5 minutes before cutting it into eight pieces.

CABBAGE CANNELLINI AND ROSEMARY SKILLET WITH QUINOA

MAKES 3 TO 4 SERVINGS NUT-FREE

1 cup (176 g) uncooked white quinoa

1 large yellow onion, diced

2 tbsp (30 ml) tamari, plus more as needed

1 tbsp (15 g) creamy Dijon mustard

1 tbsp (15 ml) balsamic vinegar

1 tsp red wine vinegar

3 tbsp (12 g) nutritional yeast

Freshly ground black pepper, plus more as needed

4 large cloves garlic, minced

8 oz (225 g) button mushrooms, thinly sliced

Leaves from 3 (5″ [12.5-cm]) sprigs rosemary, minced

½ medium-sized head green cabbage, stem and core removed and discarded, finely chopped (about 6 cups [540 g])

1½ cups (384 g) cooked or canned cannellini beans, drained and rinsed

A hearty vegetable, a bean and a grain. This is the whole food formula I stick to when cooking dinner without a recipe or any real plan, and it was the inspiration for this easy one-pan meal. It's made from simple, wholesome ingredients and ready in under 30 minutes. Humble cabbage is transformed with a few of sprigs of rosemary and a couple of splashes of tamari and balsamic vinegar. It's quick and nutritious while still being flavorful. Be sure to chop your cabbage small for best results. If you're feeling gourmet, stir some toasted almonds or walnuts into the pan and pair with a good red wine.

Start by cooking the quinoa according to the package directions. Once cooked, fluff with a fork and set it aside, covered, until needed.

Meanwhile in a large skillet, sauté the onion with a few tablespoons (about 30 ml) of water for 7 to 10 minutes, or until soft and translucent. Add water as needed to prevent burning.

In a separate small bowl, whisk together the tamari, Dijon mustard, balsamic and red wine vinegars, nutritional yeast and a pinch of black pepper. Set aside.

Now, add the garlic, mushrooms and rosemary to the skillet and cook over medium heat, stirring often, for 3 to 5 minutes, or until the mushrooms start releasing their juices. Try not to add water here as the mushrooms will eventually release their juices and you want to avoid the skillet becoming too watery.

Next, add the cabbage and beans and cook for another 3 to 5 minutes, again stirring often, until the cabbage shrinks significantly in size. Pour in the tamari mixture and stir everything together. Simmer for another 2 minutes. Taste and reseason with tamari or black pepper.

Spoon the quinoa into bowls and top with the cabbage mixture.

QUESO CRUCIFEROUS CASSEROLE AND QUESO DIP

CASSEROLE

1½ cups (300 g) uncooked brown rice

3 cups (300 g) bite-sized cauliflower florets

4 cups (284 g) bite-sized broccoli florets

1½ cups (258 g) cooked or canned black beans or pinto beans, drained and rinsed

¾ cup (86 g) gluten-free bread crumbs (optional)

QUESO SAUCE

1½ cups (255 g) peeled and chopped potato

1 cup (130 g) chopped carrot

1 cup (150 g) chopped yellow onion

¾ cup (105 g) raw cashews, soaked in hot water for 1 to 3 hours

2 to 4 jarred jalapeño slices (optional)

1½ tsp (5 g) garlic powder

1 tsp onion powder

1 tbsp + 2 tsp (7 g) nutritional yeast

1 tbsp (15 ml) fresh lemon juice

1 tbsp (15 g) Dijon mustard

1 tbsp (16 g) white miso

1 tsp apple cider vinegar

¾ tsp sea salt

½ cup (120 ml) vegetable stock

Broccoli and cauliflower are two of the healthiest whole foods and my favorite vegetables, as you can probably tell; I am seriously passionate about the cruciferous family. And here, they've never tasted better. The creamy queso sauce turns modest rice and vegetables into a winning casserole that you'll have on repeat. I've served this to many cheese lovers, and they always clean their plates. Feel free to use your bean of choice; the bread crumbs are optional but add a nice toasty flavor and texture. Add the jarred jalapeño for a little extra zip! This queso sauce is also my go-to dip when entertaining. I serve it warm with corn tortillas and a combination of roasted and raw veggies.

Start the casserole: First, make the rice according to the package directions. Once done, fluff with a fork and cover until needed.

Meanwhile, make the queso sauce: Fit a steamer basket into a large pot and fill the pot with water to just below the steamer basket. Bring to a boil. Once boiling, put the potato, carrot and onion in the basket and cover the pot. Steam the veggies for 10 to 15 minutes, or until all are very tender.

Remove the steamer basket from the pot and transfer the vegetables to a high-speed blender. You'll use the steamer basket and pot again.

Drain the cashews, discarding the soaking liquid, and add them to the blender along with the jalapeño (if using), garlic and onion powders, nutritional yeast, lemon juice, Dijon mustard, miso, vinegar, salt and stock. Blend on high speed, using your blender's tamper to help the blending process. Keep blending until the mixture is smooth.

(continued)

When the rice is cooked, preheat the oven to 400°F (200°C) and place the steamer basket back in the pot. Add more water to the pot, if needed, and bring to a boil. Once the water is boiling, place the cauliflower in the basket and cover. Steam for about 4 minutes, then add the broccoli to the basket and steam for another 2 minutes. The broccoli should be bright green and almost tender.

Transfer the steamed cauliflower and broccoli, cooked rice and beans to a 7 x 11-inch (18 x 28-cm) casserole dish. Pour the queso sauce over everything and mix to combine. Spread the mixture evenly and sprinkle the bread crumbs (if using) over the top. Lightly press the bread crumbs into the top of the casserole and bake, uncovered, for 8 to 10 minutes, or until the bread crumbs are browned and crispy. Remove from the oven and serve immediately.

NOTES

This queso sauce doubles as a crowd-pleasing nacho dip! Make the sauce with hot stock or water, pour it warm right into a bowl and serve with raw and roasted veggies, nacho chips (see how to make your own on page 46), toasted bread or warm Fabulous Lentil Flatbreads (page 149).

To put a different spin on the nacho sauce, try adding 1 teaspoon of taco seasoning mix, cumin or smoked paprika.

If you eat gluten, you can use any whole-grain bread crumbs instead of gluten-free.

TOFU SHAKSHUKA

MAKES 4 TO 6 SERVINGS 🌸 NUT–FREE

TOFU EGGS

1 (14-oz [400-g]) package firm tofu

2 tsp (3 g) nutritional yeast

1 tbsp (15 ml) fresh lemon juice

¾ tsp kala namak (black Indian salt), or sea salt

3 tbsp (45 ml) water, plus more as needed

Shakshuka is a simple one-pan meal where eggs are poached in a fragrant tomato sauce. If you follow any foodies or food bloggers on social media, you're already aware that this vibrant dish is having a moment. I must admit that I was skeptical when I first rolled up my sleeves to try a veganized version. I wasn't sure the finished product would be as eye-catching or that the tofu would perform. But it is and they did! The tofu eggs cook perfectly while nestled in the chunky tomato sauce and the fresh herbs offer a striking contrast to the warming spices. This is a beautiful brunch, lunch or dinner. Serve it with warm grains or whole-grain bread, or even with a side of steamed greens.

First make the tofu eggs: Drain the tofu and give it a squeeze over the sink to remove some excess water. Break the tofu into pieces and place them in a high-speed blender or food processor. Add the nutritional yeast, lemon juice, kala namak and water. Blend or process continuously until completely smooth. If using a high-speed blender, use your tamper to assist the blending. If using a food processor, stop and scrape down the sides often to incorporate all the ingredients. Add more water, 1 tablespoon (15 ml) at a time, if necessary to aid the blending. Your brand of tofu will determine the amount of additional liquid needed; too much water will make the tofu eggs too loose. You want the consistency to be smooth and thick. Transfer the blended mixture to a bowl and set it aside.

(continued)

VEGGIES AND TOMATOES

1 red onion, diced

1 red bell pepper, seeded, stemmed and diced

4 cloves garlic, minced

2 tsp (5 g) smoked paprika

2 tsp (5 g) ground cumin

1 tsp ground coriander

¼ tsp red pepper flakes, or to your preference

¼ tsp chili powder

½ tsp sea salt

2 tbsp (30 ml) tomato paste

2 (15-oz [425-g]) cans diced tomatoes

1 cup (170 g) cooked or canned chickpeas, drained and rinsed

FOR SERVING

Large bunch cilantro or mint

Freshly ground black pepper

Just-cooked brown rice, crusty whole-grain bread and/or steamed greens

Make the veggies and tomatoes: Preheat the oven to 400°F (200°C).

In a 10-inch (25.5-cm) oven-safe skillet or braiser, sauté the onion and bell pepper with a few tablespoons (about 30 ml) of water for 5 to 7 minutes, or until just softened.

Add the garlic, smoked paprika, cumin, coriander, red pepper flakes, chili powder, salt and tomato paste and cook for another few minutes, stirring and adding water as needed to prevent burning.

Next, add the diced tomatoes and their juices and chickpeas. Bring to a simmer and cook, uncovered, over low to medium heat for 10 minutes. Turn off the heat.

Make little wells in the surface of the tomatoes for the tofu eggs. Using a spring-release scoop or just a large spoon, scoop out about ⅓ cup (80 ml) of the tofu mixture for each "egg" and place them in the wells. You should get six to seven. Use the back of a spoon to gently spread and smooth out the tofu to make neat circles.

Bake in the oven for 25 to 30 minutes. The shakshuka should be reduced and the tofu eggs should be golden, no longer wet in the middle and slightly firm. You can pop the shakshuka under the broiler for a few minutes to give the eggs more color, if desired. Remove the shakshuka from the oven and let it rest for 10 minutes, lightly covered.

Garnish the shakshuka with fresh cilantro or mint (or both) and black pepper. To serve, use a spatula or large spoon to scoop under the eggs and transfer onto individual plates. Serve with crusty bread, warm grains or steamed greens, if desired.

SUN-DRIED TOMATO CABBAGE ROLLS WITH SUNFLOWER SEED RICOTTA

MAKES 12 CABBAGE ROLLS 🌱 NUT-FREE

CABBAGE ROLLS AND FILLING

1 (14-oz [400-g]) block extra-firm tofu

15 large green cabbage leaves (see Tips)

1 cup (150 g) finely chopped red or yellow onion

½ cup (40 g) sun-dried tomatoes (not the kind packed in oil), soaked in water for 15 minutes

8 oz (225 g) button mushrooms, thinly sliced

I was never a big fan of cabbage rolls; I thought they were a bit of a plea to use lackluster cabbage leaves. The problem was I never liked what was rolled up inside. Since going plant-based, I've had a complete change of heart. Now, I see sturdy cabbage leaves as an opportunity to neatly serve all kinds of delicious combinations. There are three components to this recipe: blanch and shock the cabbage leaves, make the ricotta filling and assemble. Cabbage rolls, in general, take a little extra time, but the yield is substantial and using a quality jarred marinara can help shorten prep. You can also make the filling ahead of time or the day before. I always suggest preparing a few more leaves than needed, in case one rips or needs patching up. Here, it's better to skip soaking the sunflower seeds to avoid adding any additional liquid to the dish. Similarly, be sure to press the tofu to remove excess water. Serve these rich and creamy cabbage rolls on their own or with warm cooked grains.

Make the cabbage rolls: First, press the tofu by wrapping the block in a clean dish towel and placing it on a level surface. Lay a cutting board on the tofu and something heavy on top, such as a cookbook or some cans of beans. Press for 20 minutes. Then, unwrap the tofu and it's ready to use.

Meanwhile, blanch and shock the cabbage leaves: Bring a large pot of water to a boil and fill a large bowl with ice water.

Submerge two cabbage leaves at a time in the boiling water for 2 to 3 minutes, or until they are flexible. Tougher leaves will need to be boiled a little longer.

(continued)

SUNFLOWER SEED RICOTTA

¾ cup (109 g) raw sunflower seeds

3 tbsp (45 ml) fresh lemon juice

3 cloves garlic, crushed and peeled

2 tsp (2 g) dried oregano

1½ tsp (4 g) chili powder

¼ tsp red pepper flakes, or to your preference

½ tsp sea salt

½ cup (120 ml) water

2½ cups (590 ml) vegan jarred marinara or My House Marinara (page 58)

Remove the leaves from the pot, using tongs—be careful, as the cabbage leaves can easily rip—and submerge them in the ice water. You can let the leaves hang out in the ice water for a minute. Then, remove them from the water and pat them dry to remove any excess water (this is important, to prevent too much water pooling in the casserole dish). Repeat with the remaining cabbage leaves.

Cut out and discard the hard stem and any heavy ribs from each cabbage leaf, creating a V shape at the base. Set aside.

Next, make the filling. In a large sauté pan, sauté the onion with a few tablespoons of water (30 ml) for 7 to 10 minutes, adding water, as needed, to prevent burning. While the onion is cooking, drain the sun-dried tomatoes well, discarding their soaking liquid and finely chop them.

Add the mushrooms and sun-dried tomatoes to the pan and continue to cook over medium heat, stirring often, for another 3 to 5 minutes, or until the mushrooms begin to shrink and release their juices. Drain off and discard any excess liquid in the pan and transfer the mixture to a medium-sized bowl. Unwrap the pressed tofu and, using your hands, finely crumble the tofu into the bowl of veggies. Mix everything together and set aside.

Make the ricotta: In a high-speed blender, combine the sunflower seeds, lemon juice, garlic, oregano, chili powder, red pepper flakes, salt and water. Blend on high speed until the mixture is as smooth as possible. Scoop the ricotta into the bowl of veggies and tofu and mix well.

Time to assemble: Spread 1 cup (240 ml) of marinara over the bottom of a 9 x 13-inch (23 x 33-cm) casserole dish or similar size.

Place a rounded ⅓ cup (90 ml) of the filling across the center of each cabbage roll. Starting at the V shape's end, pull the V together, roll the cabbage leaf over the filling once, fold in the sides and roll forward away from you into a nice bundle, like a burrito. Place the roll, seam side down, in the casserole dish. Repeat with each roll. Spoon 1 to 2 tablespoons (15 to 30 ml) of additional marinara onto each roll.

1½ cups (264 g) uncooked white quinoa

Cover the dish with tinfoil and bake for 25 minutes, then uncover and bake for another 25 minutes, or until the sauce is bubbling. Remove the casserole dish from the oven and let the rolls rest for 5 to 10 minutes. Meanwhile, when the cabbage rolls have 10 minutes left in the oven, cook the quinoa (if using) according to the package directions.

Serve the cabbage rolls on their own or on top of warm quinoa. Spoon the remaining marinara from the casserole dish onto the rolls.

TIPS FOR MAKING CABBAGE ROLLS

- *When removing the leaves from the head of cabbage, it's best to break them off from the stem or the bottom of the cabbage instead of peeling from the top. This helps prevent tears in the leaves.*

- *Remove the hard stem and veining that runs up the cabbage leaf by cutting a narrow V in the base of the leaf. If any leaves tear in the process of blanching or rolling, simply patch up the torn area with an extra leaf you've prepared.*

- *When rolling, start with the cut-out V section. Gently pull the V together and roll it forward, away from you.*

- *Cabbage rolls often run into the issue of releasing too much liquid, so to prevent soggy rolls, it's important to make sure the leaves are completely dry before making the rolls. It's also crucial to cook off or pour off any additional liquid from the filling before making the rolls. And, finally, using a thick marinara will help reduce any liquid pooling in the dish.*

- *Pressing tofu: I skip pressing tofu quite often; I think it's unnecessary in many recipes. However, in these cabbage rolls, we want to remove as much water from the ingredients as possible, so the rolls don't release too much liquid in the casserole dish as they bake.*

WARM ME UP: SOOTHING SOUPS AND STEWS

I'm from the island of Newfoundland, part of the most easterly province in Canada. The weather can be tough—dreary, windy, chilly. Every Newfoundlander knows the relief of thawing out and warming up over a steamy bowl of soup. Perhaps it's instilled in me from childhood or it's in my genes, but I can think of nothing more comforting, more healing and nurturing than a bowl of hot, homemade soup—even now while I live in subtropical Taiwan. Slurped and sopped up with a whole-grain bread, it's truly satisfying and provides a level of security that I feel deep in my bones. I depend on delicious soups and stews to nourish me when I'm unwell, comfort me when I'm homesick and to feed a crowd when I'm short on time (and ingredients) and want to cook something that tastes great.

If you're trying to incorporate more vegetables in your diet but aren't ready to dive into more complex recipes with many ingredients, bean and veggie soups are the answer. There is a soup or stew for every season in this chapter. I hope you try them all.

MY BEST CHILI

MAKES 6 SERVINGS   NUT-FREE OPTION

1 tbsp (11 g) whole black mustard seeds

1 tbsp (6 g) whole cumin seeds

1 large red onion, diced

1 (8-oz [225-g]) package tempeh

12 oz (340 g) button or cremini mushrooms

2 tsp (2 g) ground coriander

3 tbsp (23 g) chili powder

1 tsp smoked paprika

½ tsp dried oregano

½ tsp sea salt, or to taste

2 tsp (7 g) coconut sugar

1 tbsp (8 g) chile in adobo sauce, chile minced

2 tbsp (30 ml) tomato paste

8 cloves garlic, minced

1 yellow bell pepper, seeded and diced

1 red bell pepper, seeded and diced

1½ cups (258 g) cooked or canned black beans, drained and rinsed

1½ cups (384 g) cooked or canned kidney beans, drained and rinsed

½ cup (65 g) frozen corn kernels

1 (28-oz [800-g]) can diced tomatoes

1½ to 2 cups (355 to 475 ml) low-sodium vegetable stock

Optional garnishes: fresh cilantro or parsley, thinly sliced green onions, Cashew Sour Cream (recipe follows), diced avocado

I am a chili enthusiast and I love to make different versions but this chili is my all-time favorite. We start with toasted whole cumin and mustard seeds and finish with tangy sour cream. It's substantial and meaty, thanks to finely chopped tempeh and mushrooms, and it has a depth of flavor that rivals any version made with ground beef. I highly recommend topping it with a little bit of fat to balance the acidic tomatoes; if you want to skip to the sour cream, try diced avocado or the Almond Cilantro Pesto (page 46) instead. Like most chilis, this one is even better left over and freezes wonderfully.

In a large, heavy-bottomed soup pot, toast the mustard and cumin seeds over low to medium heat for 2 minutes, or until they are deeply fragrant and start to pop. Next, add the onion and ⅓ cup (80 ml) of water. The water will sizzle and spit. Sauté the onions for 7 to 10 minutes, or until the onion is soft and translucent. Add water, as needed, to prevent burning.

Meanwhile, break the tempeh into a few pieces and place it in a food processor. Process briefly until crumbly. Transfer the tempeh to a bowl. Now, place the mushrooms in the processor and pulse until finely chopped. If you want to skip the food processor, finely chop both the tempeh and mushrooms.

Add the mushrooms and crumbly tempeh to the pot along with the coriander, chili powder, paprika, oregano, salt, coconut sugar, chile in adobo and tomato paste. Stir to coat everything. Cook over medium heat for another 5 minutes, or until the mushrooms have released their juices.

Next, add the garlic and bell peppers and cook for another minute. Add the black and kidney beans, corn, diced tomatoes and 1½ cups (355 ml) of the stock, and bring to a boil. Once boiling, lower the heat to a simmer and cook, partially covered, for 1 hour, stirring often to prevent sticking. Now, remove the cover and simmer, uncovered, until thickened, 5 to 10 minutes. If you want to thin the chili or find it is sticking too much, add an additional ½ cup (120 ml) of stock.

Taste and reseason with salt and black pepper, if needed. Divide among bowls and garnish with parsley, cilantro, or green onion and Cashew Sour Cream and/or avocado.

CASHEW SOUR CREAM

MAKES 1 CUP (250 G)

1 cup (140 g) raw cashews, soaked in hot water for 1 to 3 hours

1 tbsp (15 ml) apple cider vinegar or fresh lemon juice

1 tsp Dijon mustard

¼ tsp sea salt

½ cup (120 ml) water, plus more if needed to thin

Cashew sour cream is a plant-based staple. It's versatile, easy to make, and can be used in any recipe or in any way you would use traditional sour cream. It keeps in the fridge for up to a week.

Drain the cashews, discarding the soaking liquid, and place them in a high-speed blender along with the vinegar, Dijon mustard, salt and water. Blend on high speed until completely smooth, adding more water, if needed, to achieve a creamy consistency.

PLANT-BASED DELICIOUS

ROASTED RED PEPPER SOUP WITH HERBED PUMPKIN SEED CROUTONS

MAKES 4 SERVINGS   NUT-FREE OPTION

SOUP

4 large red bell peppers (800 g), or 1¼ cups packed (225 g) roasted peppers

1 small red onion, diced (1 cup [150 g])

4 cloves garlic, minced

1 tsp smoked paprika

1 tsp dried oregano

¼ tsp dried thyme

Pinch of cayenne pepper or red pepper flakes, or to your preference

¾ tsp sea salt, or to taste

2 tbsp (30 ml) tomato paste

1 small russet potato, peeled, diced small (¾ cup [128 g])

3 cups (710 ml) low-sodium vegetable stock, plus more as needed

¼ cup (36 g) raw almonds, soaked in water overnight or for 6 to 8 hours, or (35 g) raw cashews, soaked in hot water for 1 to 3 hours

2 to 3 tbsp (30 to 45 ml) fresh lemon juice, plus more as needed

Freshly ground black pepper

Roasted red pepper anything is always a yes for me. The intense, sweet and charred flavor can completely reinvent even the simplest dish. This delightful soup is smooth and a little smoky, tangy and nutty. The flavor of home-roasted red peppers cannot be beat by any jarred variety. It's worth all the effort and will have your kitchen smelling like a bistro. I've used starchy russet potatoes to thicken the soup, as well as soaked almonds or cashews. Feel free to omit the nuts to make this a veg-only soup. I like to double batch this recipe and freeze leftovers—this way, I only have to roast the peppers once!

First, roast your peppers: Preheat the oven to 450°F (230°C). Line a large baking sheet with parchment paper. Place the whole peppers on the prepared baking sheet. Roast the peppers in the oven for 45 to 60 minutes, rotating every 15 to 20 minutes until all sides are charred. Remove the peppers from the oven and place them in a heatproof bowl. Cover with a plate and let the peppers steam for 20 to 30 minutes—this helps loosen their skins. Once cool enough to handle, peel the peppers and remove and discard the stem, core and seeds. Now, your peppers are ready. You will be reusing the baking sheet. Lower the temperature to 300°F (150°C).

Make the soup: In a soup pot, sauté the onion with a few tablespoons (about 30 ml) of water for 7 to 10 minutes, or until translucent. Add more water, as needed, to prevent burning.

Now, add the garlic, smoked paprika, oregano, thyme, cayenne pepper, salt, tomato paste and potato. Stir to combine and cook for another minute.

Add the stock and bring to a boil. Once boiling, turn the heat to low, partially cover, and simmer for 10 to 12 minutes, or until the potato is tender. Turn off the heat.

(continued)

HERBED PUMPKIN SEED CROUTONS

1 cup (140 g) pumpkin seeds

1 tbsp (15 ml) red wine vinegar

1 tsp pure maple syrup

1 tsp tamari

1 tbsp (4 g) nutritional yeast

¾ tsp dried oregano

¾ tsp dried tarragon

¾ tsp dried basil

1 tsp dried thyme

1 tsp garlic powder

Pinch of freshly ground black pepper

¼ tsp sea salt

Meanwhile, make the croutons: Line the large baking sheet with fresh parchment paper. Put the pumpkin seeds in a medium-sized bowl. In a smaller separate bowl, whisk together the vinegar, maple syrup, tamari, nutritional yeast, oregano, tarragon, basil, thyme, garlic powder, pepper and salt until a paste is formed. Pour the paste over the pumpkin seeds and toss until all the pumpkin seeds are coated. Transfer the seeds to the prepared baking sheet and spread them out in a single layer. Bake for 10 minutes. Flip the seeds around to break up any clumps and bake for another 7 to 8 minutes. The pumpkin seeds should just be developing color and be dry to the touch. Remove them from the oven and let them cool completely.

Back to the soup. Drain the nuts, discarding their soaking liquid, and place them in a blender along with the roasted red peppers and 2 tablespoons (30 ml) of the lemon juice. Carefully transfer the soup to the blender. Blend for 1 to 2 minutes, or until silky smooth. Be sure not to fill the blender beyond two-thirds full and leave a little gap to let steam escape. Blend in batches, if needed.

Taste and reseason the soup with salt, pepper or more lemon juice, as needed. Pour the soup into bowls right from the blender or transfer the soup back to the pot to keep warm. When ready to serve, ladle the soup into bowls and top with the herbed pumpkin seed croutons. Keep the remaining croutons in a cool, dry place for up to a month.

CURRIED SQUASH AND APPLE SOUP WITH ALMONDS

1 large yellow onion, diced

1 Granny smith apple, peeled, cored and chopped

3 cloves garlic, minced

1 tbsp (5 g) finely grated fresh ginger

1 tsp mild curry powder

1½ tsp (3 g) garam masala

¾ tsp sea salt, or to taste

1 small to medium-sized butternut squash (about 2 lb [905 g]), peeled, seeded and chopped into 1″ (2.5-cm) pieces (6 to 7 cups)

4 cups (946 ml) low-sodium vegetable stock

1 tbsp (15 ml) fresh lemon juice

2 tsp (10 ml) pure maple syrup

¼ cup (36 g) raw almonds, soaked overnight or for 8 hours (optional)

GARNISH

Toasted pumpkin seeds or sliced almonds

Butternut squash is clever and convenient—it plays well with so many other plant foods, herbs and spices. It's an ingredient I experiment with a lot, but it's exceptional when used in a curry soup. You can make this soup with or without the almonds, but with will result in a creamier consistency and more complex, nutty flavor. The healthy fats from the almonds also help with the absorption of the beta-carotene from the squash, an essential nutrient for your immune system. Be sure to use a mild curry powder unless you like heat.

In a soup pot, sauté the onion and apple in about ¼ cup (60 ml) of water for 7 to 10 minutes, or until the onion is translucent. Add water, a few tablespoons (about 30 ml) at a time, as needed, to prevent burning.

Now, add the garlic, ginger, curry powder, garam masala and salt. Stir and cook for another minute.

Add the squash and stock. Bring to a boil. Once boiling, turn the heat to low and simmer, partially covered, for 25 to 30 minutes. The squash will be very tender and start falling apart. Turn off the heat and stir in the lemon juice and maple syrup.

Drain the almonds, discarding their soaking liquid, and transfer them and the soup to a high-speed blender, being careful not to overfill, and blend until completely smooth. Do this in batches, if needed. Taste and reseason with salt as needed.

You can serve the soup right from the blender or return it to the pot to keep warm. Serve the soup garnished with toasted pumpkin seeds.

> ### NOTES
>
> *For a lighter, nut-free but still delicious soup, omit the almonds.*
>
> *You can replace the butternut with any other winter squash, or the almonds with cashews.*

PROVENÇAL CABBAGE AND POTATO STEW WITH WHITE BEANS

MAKES 4 SERVINGS   NUT-FREE

1 large onion, diced

1 carrot, diced

1 celery rib, diced

3 cloves garlic, minced

4 tsp (3 g) herbes de Provence

¼ tsp smoked paprika

⅛ tsp ground allspice

Pinch of red pepper flakes

21 oz (600 g) Yukon Gold potatoes (about 4 potatoes), peeled and diced

5 cups (1.2 L) vegetable stock

½ medium-sized head green cabbage, shredded or finely chopped (5 to 6 cups [450 to 540 g])

1½ cups (273 g) cooked or canned navy or (384 g) cannellini beans, drained and rinsed

1 tbsp (16 ml) white miso

1 tbsp (15 ml) fresh lemon juice

Salt and freshly ground black pepper

Cabbage is one of the cheaper vegetables, but we sometimes think of *cheap* as meaning "of inferior quality." Not cabbage. Despite its ho-hum reputation, cabbage is also outrageously nutritious, boasting loads of cancer-fighting compounds and antioxidants. So, if you're on a budget and looking to increase the nutrient density of your meals, cabbage is a fitting place to start. This wintery stew is made thick by blending half of the soup—my favorite stew trick—before the cabbage is added. You can toss in any other root veg—parsnip and turnip work well. Be sure to cut the cabbage small for even cooking and a more pleasant slurping experience. Make the Cabbage Cannellini and Rosemary Skillet (page 104) with the other half of your cabbage.

In a soup pot, sauté the onion, carrot and celery in ¼ cup (60 ml) of water for about 10 minutes, or until the onion is translucent. Add water, as needed, to prevent burning.

Next, add the garlic, herbes de Provence, smoked paprika, allspice and red pepper flakes and sauté for another minute while stirring.

Add the potatoes and vegetable stock and bring to a boil. Once boiling, turn the heat to low and simmer, partially covered, for 20 minutes, or until the potatoes are tender.

Transfer a little more than half of the soup (a mixture of the broth and veggies) to a blender and blend until smooth. Return the blended soup to the pot.

Now, add the cabbage and beans to the soup and simmer, partially covered, for 10 minutes, or until the cabbage is tender. Remove about 1 cup (240 ml) of the soup and place it in a bowl with the miso and lemon. Whisk together until the miso is dissolved and return to pot. Stir and taste and season with salt and pepper, as needed.

Divide among bowls and serve on its own or with warm, crusty bread.

BUTTERNUT SQUASH DAHL WITH CASHEW MILK AND KALE

MAKES 4 SERVINGS

1 tbsp (11 g) whole black mustard seeds

1 tbsp (6 g) whole cumin seeds

1 red onion, diced

½ tsp sea salt, plus more to taste

3 cloves garlic, minced

1 tsp ground coriander

1 tsp ground turmeric

¼ tsp red pepper flakes, or to your preference

⅛ tsp ground cardamom

Several grinds of black pepper, or to taste

3 cups (400 g) 1″ (2.5-cm) chunks peeled butternut squash

1 cup (190 g) dried split red lentils

1 (15-oz [425-g]) can diced tomatoes

3½ cups (830 ml) low-sodium vegetable stock, divided

½ cup (70 g) raw cashews, soaked in hot water for 1 to 3 hours

1 cup (67 g) finely chopped kale (optional)

Juice of ½ lime

FOR SERVING (OPTIONAL)

Cooked brown rice, quinoa or millet

I find it hard to make the same meal twice; I always want to fiddle with some ingredient or try something new, but I happily keep this dahl in consistent rotation. It's filling and flavorful and will warm you up right down to your toes. Whole spices, butternut squash and protein-rich red lentils are simmered together and then finished with a creamy cashew milk and a nip of lime juice. The kale is optional but is finely chopped, so kale naysayers will barely notice it. This might be one of our favorite meals—we never have leftovers. You can enjoy this dahl on its own or serve it with warm brown rice.

In a heavy-bottomed soup pot, toast the mustard seeds and cumin over low to medium heat for 2 minutes, or until fragrant and they start to pop.

Add the onion, salt and ¼ cup (60 ml) of water (it will sizzle and spit), and sauté for 7 to 10 minutes, or until the onion is translucent. Add more water, as needed, to prevent burning.

Add the garlic, coriander, turmeric, red pepper flakes, cardamom and black pepper and cook for another 30 seconds. Add the squash and stir to coat in the spices.

Now, pour in the red lentils, diced tomatoes and 2½ cups (590 ml) of the vegetable stock. Bring to a boil. Once boiling, turn the heat to low, partially cover and simmer for 25 minutes, or until the squash is falling apart and the lentils are very tender, even disintegrating into the broth.

Meanwhile, pour the remaining cup (240 ml) of vegetable stock into a blender. Drain the cashews, discarding the soaking liquid, add to the blender and blend until completely smooth.

Once the lentils and squash are cooked, pour in the cashew milk and add the kale (if using). Simmer over low heat for another 2 to 3 minutes, or until thickened and the kale is bright green. Add the lime juice, then taste and reseason with salt and pepper, as needed. Spoon into bowls and serve on its own or with just-cooked whole grains.

ESSENTIAL TWO-LENTIL SOUP

MAKES 3 TO 4 SERVINGS　　NUT-FREE

1 medium-sized onion, diced

1 large carrot, diced

2 celery ribs, diced

4 cloves garlic, minced

2 tsp (4 g) ground coriander

1½ tsp (3 g) garam masala

1 tsp ground cumin

1 tsp ground fennel seeds

½ tsp ground turmeric

Pinch of cayenne pepper (optional)

Several grinds of black pepper, or to taste

½ tsp sea salt, or to taste

1 medium-sized sweet potato, peeled and diced into ½" (1.3-cm) cubes

½ cup (95 g) dried split red lentils

½ cup (90 g) dried green lentils

4 cups (946 ml) low-sodium vegetable stock, plus more if needed

2 tsp (10 ml) ginger juice (from about a 1½" [4-cm] knob fresh ginger); see page 133 for how to make ginger juice

1 tbsp (15 ml) fresh lemon juice

1 tsp tamari

1 cup packed (40 g) baby spinach or (67 g) finely chopped kale (optional)

I have a soft spot for lentils—they're such a laid-back legume. They don't need soaking, they cook rather quickly and they work in almost any dish—salad, pasta, casserole or soup. For me, a good lentil soup is necessary to have in your home kitchen repertoire, especially if you live in a place where the arrival of winter really sends a shock through your system. And this is my essential lentil soup. It's made with two types of lentils—split red lentils and green lentils—for texture, and is paired with warming, healing spices. Double the recipe and freeze portions for an easy grab-and-go lunch.

In a soup pot, sauté the onion, carrot and celery in ¼ cup (60 ml) of water for 7 to 10 minutes. Add water as needed to prevent burning.

Next, add the garlic, coriander, garam masala, cumin, fennel seeds, turmeric, cayenne, black pepper and salt, and cook for another 30 seconds, stirring. Now, add the sweet potato and both types of lentils. Stir to coat everything in the spices.

Add the stock and bring to a boil. Once boiling, turn the heat down to low and simmer, covered, for 30 minutes. The veggies should be tender, and the red lentils should disintegrate into the broth.

Turn off the heat and add the ginger and lemon juices, tamari and spinach (if using), and let the soup rest for a few minutes until the greens are wilted. Taste and reseason with salt and black pepper as needed. Ladle the soup into bowls and serve.

CARROT TURMERIC AND GINGER SOUP

MAKES 4 SERVINGS • NUT-FREE OPTION

3 cups (450 g) diced yellow onion
(2 medium-sized onions)

3½ cups (455 g) diced carrot
(3 large carrots)

1 tsp sea salt, or to taste

½ tsp ground cumin

½ tsp ground turmeric

3 grinds of black pepper, plus more
as needed

4 cups (946 ml) low-sodium
vegetable stock

¼ cup (35 g) raw cashews or
sunflower seeds

2 tsp (10 ml) fresh ginger juice
(from about a 1½" [4-cm] knob
fresh ginger); (see Note below)

Juice of ½ lemon

OPTIONAL GARNISH

Herbed Pumpkin Seed Croutons
(page 122), vegan yogurt or
Cashew Sour Cream (page 120)

FOR SERVING
(OPTIONAL)

Buckwheat Bread (page 20)

I've always preferred thick, pureed soups over brothy ones, and this warming soup never disappoints—it's modest but has a gourmet feel. The anti-inflammatory and revitalizing power of ginger and turmeric combined is hard to beat—it's a match made in health heaven—and I keep this soup on standby when I feel a cold brewing or someone in the house is sniffling. Its simplicity, in both ingredients and preparation, makes it even more wonderful.

In a soup pot, sauté the onions and carrots with the salt and ⅓ cup (80 ml) of water for 15 minutes, or until the onions are very soft and translucent. Stir often and add water, a couple of tablespoons (about 30 ml) at a time, as needed, to prevent burning.

Next, add the cumin, turmeric and pepper, and cook, stirring, for another 30 seconds. Pour in the stock and bring everything to a boil. Once boiling, turn the heat down to low and simmer over low to medium heat, partially covered, for 20 minutes, or until the carrots are very tender. Halfway through, toss the cashews into the soup.

Turn off the heat and carefully transfer the soup to a high-speed blender, add the ginger and lemon juices, then blend on high speed until the soup is completely smooth and creamy. Taste and reseason with salt and pepper, as needed, and pour directly into bowls from the blender or pour back into the pot and cover to keep warm.

I love topping this soup with Herbed Pumpkin Seed Croutons (page 122), but you can also add a swirl of vegan yogurt or Cashew Sour Cream (page 120) and serve with Toasted Buckwheat Bread (page 20).

HOW TO MAKE GINGER JUICE

Ginger juice has a cleaner, brighter and less bitter taste than minced ginger. And although not always necessary, in this soup, I like to add just the juice. Juice your fresh ginger by grating it on a rasp or small handheld grater, then squeeze the juice out of the pulp. Discard the pulp and save the juice. You can also use a juicer, if you have one.

WINTER VEGETABLE STEW WITH CHICKPEAS

1 large yellow onion, diced

2 medium-sized carrots, diced

2 celery ribs, thinly sliced

5 cloves garlic, minced

2½ tsp (7 g) dried thyme

2½ tsp (3 g) dried rosemary

½ tsp ground sage

¼ tsp red pepper flakes, or to your preference

2 tbsp (30 ml) tomato paste

1 beefsteak tomato, diced

½ small rutabaga, peeled and chopped in ¾" (4-cm) cubes

1 medium-sized sweet potato, peel on, chopped into ¾" (4-cm) cubes

2 Yukon Gold potatoes, peel on, chopped into ¾" (4-cm) cubes

⅓ cup (22 g) nutritional yeast

1½ cups (255 g) cooked or canned chickpeas, drained and rinsed

5 cups (1.2 L) low-sodium vegetable stock

Freshly ground black pepper

2 tbsp (30 ml) low-sodium tamari or soy sauce

4 tsp (20 ml) red wine vinegar

When I was growing up, stew was always made to use up leftover root veggies and scraps of meat from big holiday meals—Thanksgiving, Christmas and New Year's. When I gave up meat, my mom started making a separate pot of stew for me, one without a ham bone or turkey. It was simple but wholesome, and that stew, which was more like a soup, is what I think about whenever I make my own root vegetable stew. I picture my mom in an apron, stirring a large soup pot. This stew is reminiscent of my mom's but is different (and better . . . sorry, Mom) in a lot of ways. Most notably, it's made thick without any roux or added flour, but by blending a portion of the soup. This way, you can control how thick or thin you want it. I've also added a nice serving of nutritional yeast and tamari for more umami flavor.

In a large soup pot, sauté the onion, carrots and celery with ¼ cup (60 ml) of water for 10 minutes, or until the onion is translucent. Stir often and add water, a couple of tablespoons (about 30 ml) at a time, as needed, to prevent burning.

Add the garlic, thyme, rosemary, sage, red pepper flakes and tomato paste. Stir and sauté for 1 minute. Next add the tomato, rutabaga, sweet and Yukon Gold potatoes and nutritional yeast. Stir to coat everything in the herbs and nutritional yeast, and cook for another 2 minutes.

Now, add the chickpeas and vegetable stock, and bring to a boil. Once boiling, turn the heat down to low and simmer for 30 to 35 minutes, partially covered, or until the veggies are tender.

Turn off the heat. Add the black pepper, tamari and vinegar, and stir. Now, transfer about 3 cups (710 ml) of the soup (broth, veggies and chickpeas) to a blender and blend until smooth. You can also add less or more, depending how thick you like it. Add the blended mixture back to the pot. Taste and add more vinegar, tamari and/or black pepper if needed. Ladle into bowls and serve.

TOMATO BISQUE WITH BRAZIL NUTS

MAKES 4 TO 6 SERVINGS

1 small yellow onion, diced

½ tsp sea salt, or to taste

3 large cloves garlic, minced

Pinch of red pepper flakes, or to your preference

2 (28-oz [800-g]) cans diced tomatoes

¾ cup (175 ml) low-sodium vegetable stock or water, plus more if needed

2 Medjool dates, pits removed

6 Brazil nuts

1 tbsp (15 ml) fresh lemon juice

1 tsp dried basil, or large handful of fresh

Freshly ground black pepper

I can cozy up with a good bowl of tomato soup any time of year, even in the sweltering summer heat. This zippy tomato soup is really a dream—it's terribly easy and has superfood status, thanks to Brazil nuts. These large nuts, rich in immunity-boosting selenium, give this soup a creamy texture and a nutritional boost. It has a "This is vegan?!" effect where your guests just won't believe it's dairy-free, oil-free and conveniently made with canned tomatoes. You can also reduce the stock and make it more like a thick tomato sauce to toss with cooked pasta.

In a soup pot, sauté the onion with the salt and a few tablespoons (about 30 ml) of water for 7 to 10 minutes, or until translucent. Add water, as needed, to prevent burning. Now, add the garlic and red pepper flakes and cook for another 30 seconds.

Add the diced tomatoes and all their juices, stock or water and pitted dates and bring to a boil. Lower the heat to a rapid simmer and cover. Simmer, covered, for 10 minutes.

Turn off the heat and transfer the soup to a high-speed blender. Add the Brazil nuts, lemon juice and basil and blend on high speed for 1 to 2 minutes, or until the soup is completely smooth and creamy. You'll likely need to do the blending in two batches to not overfill the blender. Be sure to leave the ventilation cap open or lay a clean dish towel over the slightly ajar lid so the steam can escape from the blender.

Add more stock or water if you like a thinner soup. Taste and reseason with salt and pepper as needed. Pour into bowls right from the blender or transfer back to the pot to keep warm. Like any pureed soup, you can toss in some cooked whole grains, beans or greens to make this a chunkier soup and a more filling meal.

AT HOME GOURMET: IMPRESSIVE AND EASY ENTRÉES

Comfort food has a place in every setting—lazy nights in and even fancy nights out. This chapter was inspired by some of my favorite restaurant experiences that I wanted to recreate at home and by my unwavering posture that "plant-based" does not mean "plain" or "pedestrian." These are supernutritious and comforting meals mindfully plated with a touch of posh.

Because it's not just what we eat, it's how we eat that matters, too. Setting aside a little extra time every now and then to sit down to a special meal is important. Lay out the good plates, spread the fancy tablecloth, light a candle. Even if it's just for yourself. It makes a difference and might be the restorative experience you're looking for.

MOROCCAN POTPIES WITH ALMOND PASTRY

MAKES 5 (12-OUNCE [355-ML]) PERSONAL POTPIES, OR 1 (9- OR 10-INCH [23- OR 25.5-CM]) POTPIE

½ cup (75 g) diced onion

1½ cups (195 g) diced carrot

½ cup (50 g) diced celery

½ tsp sea salt, or more to taste

5 large cloves garlic, minced

1½ tsp (4 g) ground cumin

1½ tsp (3 g) ground coriander

1 tsp ground cinnamon

¼ tsp ground turmeric

¼ tsp red pepper flakes

¼ tsp freshly ground black pepper

1 red bell pepper, seeded, stemmed and diced

4 cups (400 g) bite-sized cauliflower florets

1½ cups (12 oz [355 ml]) passata or tomato sauce

1¼ cups (296 ml) water or vegetable stock

1 cup (130 g) frozen green peas or (170 g) cooked or canned chickpeas, drained and rinsed

3 tbsp (45 ml) stirred almond butter

Juice of ½ lemon

1 packed cup (40 g) baby spinach

1 batch Pizza Crust (page 82)

There's something special about being served your own potpie. It feels personalized, made just for you. And that's exactly how I like to make guests feel—warm, welcomed and loved. Despite looking as though they take a good bit of work, these potpies are rather straightforward. The pastry crust (which is also the Pizza Crust on page 82) crisps perfectly in the oven and the filling is so good you can just make it on its own and serve it with cooked grains. If you're hoping to make something in advance for a dinner party, you can assemble these potpies and place them in the fridge for up to four hours. Remove the ramekins from the fridge and let them come to room temperature before placing them in the oven.

The size of your ramekins is particularly important for this recipe. I use 1½-cup (355-ml) ramekins that measure 4½ inches (11.5 cm) in diameter and 2¼ inches (5.5 cm) in height. If you have differently sized ramekins or cocottes, your yield will be different. You can also make one larger potpie in an 8-cup (1.9-L), 9- or 10-inch (23- or 25.5-cm) pie dish. The crust is quite forgiving so you can roll it thinner (but it will be a little more fragile) or a little thicker to accommodate your needs.

In a large sauté pan, sauté the onion, carrot, celery and salt in ¼ cup (60 ml) of water for 10 minutes. Stir often and add water, a few tablespoons (about 30 ml) at a time, as needed, to prevent burning.

Add the garlic, cumin, coriander, cinnamon, turmeric, red pepper flakes and black pepper, and cook for another 30 seconds.

(continued)

Add the bell pepper and cauliflower, and stir to coat everything in the spices. Pour in the passata and water and bring to a simmer. Once simmering, cover and cook for 20 minutes, stirring a couple of times throughout, or until the cauliflower is fork-tender. Turn the heat to low and add the green peas and almond butter. Stir vigorously until the almond butter melts into the mixture. If the mixture is more watery than thick, simmer, uncovered, for a couple of minutes until the liquid reduces. Add the lemon juice and spinach, and stir again. Remove from the heat, taste and reseason with salt and pepper and cover until needed. Preheat the oven to 400°F (200°C).

Next, make the pastry for the crust and roll it out into a rough 9½-inch (24-cm) circle, according to the directions on page 82. If using ramekins, invert three ramekins upside down on the dough and trace around each with a sharp knife. Rework the remaining dough and roll it out again to fit two ramekins on top to trace the final two crusts. Use the top of a piping tip to pierce a hole in the middle of each crust or simply score the dough with a knife. Use a fork to score around the edges of each potpie crust. If making one large potpie, roll out the dough into a rough 9½-inch (24-cm) circle and pierce three holes in the middle with the piping tip.

Spoon the veggie mixture into each ramekin until full and flush with the top. Gently lay a crust on each ramekin and lightly press on the rim of the ramekin so the crust sticks in place. If using a pie plate, fill with the veggie mixture and then lay the crust on top, making sure it is in contact with the filling, and then, using a fork or your fingers, gently fold or crimp the edges, pressing it against the lip of the plate.

Bake the ramekins for 18 to 20 minutes, or until the crust is golden. If making a larger potpie, bake for 23 to 25 minutes. They're done when the crust is golden and maybe starting to brown on the edges. Remove from the oven and let rest for a few minutes before serving. I like to pair these potpies with a simple side salad.

ROASTED MUSHROOMS AND WILD RICE WITH ALMOND MILK

MAKES 3 TO 4 SERVINGS

1 cup (180 g) uncooked wild rice blend

20 oz (567 g) mixed mushrooms—roughly equal amounts oyster, button and cremini

3 tbsp (45 ml) balsamic vinegar

2 tsp (10 ml) tamari

Several grinds of black pepper

1 large onion, diced

1 large carrot, diced

2 celery ribs, diced

1 small bunch Swiss chard, stems thinly sliced and leaves finely chopped, stems and leaves separated

¾ tsp sea salt, divided

3 cloves garlic, minced

1½ tsp (1 g) fresh thyme, or ½ dried, plus more for garnish

1½ tsp (1 g) minced fresh rosemary leaves, or ½ tsp dried

¼ tsp red pepper flakes, or to your preference

⅛ tsp ground nutmeg, plus a pinch more for the almond milk

1 tbsp (4 g) nutritional yeast

1 cup (145 g) raw almonds, soaked overnight or for 6 to 8 hours

2½ cups (590 ml) water

1½ tsp (8 ml) red wine vinegar

If you're like me, you automatically reach for the sauté pan when cooking mushrooms, but here the sheet pan does an even better job. This elegant recipe was inspired by a stunning slow cooker recipe by Tieghan Gerard from Half Baked Harvest (https://www.halfbakedharvest.com). It's a veganized version made a little luxurious with homemade almond milk. I especially love preparing the mushrooms by tearing them with my hands instead of using a knife—it's always grounding to get your hands involved. Fresh thyme and rosemary deliver the best flavor, but dried can be used instead. Soaking the almonds is optional but a good idea if you have time.

Cook the wild rice according to the package directions. When it's done, fluff with a fork, cover and set aside until needed.

Preheat the oven to 400°F (200°C) and line a large baking sheet with parchment paper.

Break or tear the mushrooms into pieces of various sizes and place them in a large bowl. Pour the balsamic vinegar and tamari over the mushrooms and toss to coat. Add some black pepper and toss again. Spread out the mushrooms on the prepared baking sheet and roast for 25 minutes, flipping and mixing halfway through.

Meanwhile, in a soup pot, sauté the onion, carrot, celery, Swiss chard stems and ½ teaspoon of the salt with ¼ cup (60 ml) of water for 15 minutes, or until the veggies are all very tender. Add water as needed, a few tablespoons (about 30 ml) at a time, and stir often to prevent sticking.

(continued)

Add the garlic, thyme, rosemary, red pepper flakes, nutmeg and nutritional yeast, and cook for another 30 seconds. Stir in the Swiss chard leaves and turn off the heat.

Drain the almonds, discarding the soaking liquid, and place them in a high-speed blender with the 2½ cups (590 ml) of water, the remaining ¼ teaspoon of salt and a pinch of ground nutmeg. Blend on high speed for 1 minute. The milk should be slightly warmed. Strain the almond milk, using a nut milk bag or fine-mesh strainer lined with cheesecloth. Set the milk aside and save the almond pulp for another use (I like to add it to my next batch of Three-Grain Slow-Cooker Porridge, page 32).

Add the cooked rice, about three-quarters of the roasted mushrooms and 1¼ cups (295 ml) of the almond milk to the pot of veggies. Stir and bring the mixture to a gentle simmer over low heat until heated throughout and the chard is wilted. Stir in the red wine vinegar and turn off the heat.

Divide among bowls and garnish each bowl with the remaining roasted mushrooms and thyme. Pour a little of the remaining almond milk into the bottom of each bowl so it swirls around the rice, mushrooms and vegetables.

> NOTES
>
> *If Swiss chard isn't available, use baby spinach instead.*
>
> *To save time, you can make the almond milk and rice ahead of time and keep them in the fridge until needed.*

CREAM OF CORN RISOTTO WITH MARINATED TEMPEH

MAKES 3 TO 4 SERVINGS ⊛ NUT-FREE OPTION

MARINATED TEMPEH

1 (8-oz [225-g]) package tempeh

¼ cup (60 ml) low-sodium tamari

3 tbsp (45 ml) balsamic vinegar

2 tsp (10 ml) red wine vinegar

2 tbsp (30 ml) pure maple syrup

2 large cloves garlic, minced

½ tsp smoked paprika

½ tsp dried basil

2 tbsp (30 ml) water, plus more if needed

RISOTTO AND BROCCOLI

1¼ cups (225 g) uncooked short-grain brown rice

3 cups (710 ml) low-sodium vegetable stock

½ tsp sea salt, or to taste

1 batch Corn Hollandaise (page 27)

1 large head broccoli, cut into 1½" to 2" (4- to 5-cm) florets

OPTIONAL GARNISH

Sprouts or microgreens

Risotto tempts like no other dish, but it can also be intimidating to make. I set out to create a risotto that was healthy and more home chef-friendly with some shortcuts—a lot of shortcuts—but with all the creaminess you're hoping for. I've used chewy short-grain brown rice instead of Arborio, and I've made it creamy not by consistently stirring but by cooking it longer with more broth and whisking in rich Corn Hollandaise (page 27). The method of preparation is by no means traditional, it's anything but; however, the results are outstanding. Paired with a marinated and simmered tempeh, this dish is a lovely meal to serve guests or to prepare for a special night in.

Start by marinating the tempeh: Cut the block of tempeh in half and then cut each tempeh half into eight triangles (for a total of sixteen triangles). In a shallow dish with a cover, combine the tamari, balsamic and red wine vinegar, maple syrup, garlic, paprika, basil and water, and mix. Place the tempeh in the dish, then cover and flip back and forth until all the tempeh is coated. Set the tempeh aside until needed and rotate the container every now and then to evenly marinate it.

Now, make the risotto: Rinse the rice in a fine-mesh strainer and place it in a medium-sized pot with the vegetable stock and salt. Cover and bring to a boil. Once boiling, turn the heat down to low and simmer, covered, over low heat for the recommended time on the package plus 5 minutes. This will usually be around 50 minutes. While the rice is cooking, make the Corn Hollandaise per the directions on page 27.

(continued)

AT HOME GOURMET: IMPRESSIVE AND EASY ENTRÉES

Once the rice is done—it should be a little overcooked—add the corn hollandaise to the pot of rice and mix vigorously until creamy. Remove from the heat and cover until needed. The risotto will thicken and set as it rests in the pot.

Now, transfer the tempeh and all its marinade to a medium-sized sauté pan or pot and bring to a simmer. Cook over low to medium heat, stirring occasionally, for 5 to 7 minutes. The marinade will thicken. Add water, if needed, to prevent sticking. Cover and remove from the heat.

Meanwhile, fit a steamer basket into a medium-sized pot, fill with water to just below the basket and bring to a boil. Add the broccoli, cover and steam for 3 to 5 minutes, or until bright green and vibrant.

Taste the risotto and reseason with salt and pepper, as needed. Divide the risotto among bowls and top with the tempeh and broccoli. Finish each bowl with sprouts (if using).

NOTES

To shorten the prep time, you can make the corn hollandaise and the tempeh marinade the day before and keep them in the fridge.

For a nut-free option, make the corn hollandaise with sunflower seeds instead of cashews.

Sometimes, when I want to make the broccoli a little more exciting, I like to blanch and shock and then roast it. Here's how: preheat the oven to 400°F (200°C). Bring a large pot of water to a boil and fill a large bowl with ice water. Submerge the broccoli florets in the boiling water and boil for 2 to 3 minutes, or until bright green. Carefully remove the florets, using a slotted spoon, and plunge them into the ice water. This freezes the cooking process, so the broccoli stays vibrant. Set aside in the ice water for 5 minutes until completely cooled. Then, drain well and transfer the broccoli to a clean dish towel to dry. Spread the florets in a single layer on a parchment-lined baking sheet. Bake for 20 minutes, flipping halfway through, until the broccoli just begins to char on the tips, then serve.

FABULOUS LENTIL FLATBREADS WITH ROASTED VEGGIES AND TAHINI LEMON SAUCE

MAKES 5 FLATBREADS · NUT-FREE

LENTIL FLATBREADS

1 cup (190 g) dried split red lentils

1¾ cups (414 ml) water

½ tsp onion powder

½ tsp garlic powder

A few grinds of black pepper

½ tsp sea salt

1 tbsp (15 ml) fresh lemon juice

VEGETABLES

4 heaping cups (450 g) 1″ (2.5-cm) cauliflower florets

1 large red onion, cut into 1″ (2.5-cm) wedges

1 red bell pepper, seeded, stemmed and cut into strips

2 handfuls of cherry tomatoes

1 tbsp (4 g) nutritional yeast

1 tsp dried oregano

1 tsp ground cumin

1 tsp ground coriander

½ tsp sea salt

Pinch of freshly ground black pepper

Juice of ½ lemon

2 cups (40 g) baby arugula

1 avocado, pitted and peeled, thinly sliced

It's rare that a recipe is easy, made from everyday ingredients and beautiful once plated, but here we have it! In this recipe, it's the transformation of dried lentils that's truly remarkable. Split red lentils are soaked and blended into a frothy batter before being cooked like a pancake, then topped with lightly seasoned veggies. I still get excited every time I blend up the batter. Sometimes, I eat these proper-like with a knife and fork, and other times, I scoop them up with my hands and eat them like a giant taco. Chef's choice! This recipe could easily have been in the "Ashley's Favorites" chapter. I love it.

For the flatbreads: In a medium-sized bowl, combine the lentils and water and set them aside to soak for 1 to 3 hours.

When ready to cook the flatbreads, preheat the oven to 425°F (220°C), line a baking sheet with parchment paper and start the vegetables: In a large bowl, combine the cauliflower, onion, bell pepper and tomatoes.

In a small bowl, mix together the nutritional yeast, oregano, cumin, coriander, salt and pepper. Squeeze the lemon juice over the veggies in the bowl and toss to coat. Then, sprinkle half of the spice mixture over the veggies and toss to coat. Next, sprinkle the remaining spice mixture and toss again. Spread out the veggies on the prepared pan and roast in the oven for 30 to 35 minutes, or until tender and beginning to char on the edges.

(continued)

TAHINI SAUCE

¼ cup (60 g) stirred tahini

2 tbsp (30 ml) fresh lemon juice

1 clove garlic, minced

¼ tsp sea salt

3 to 4 tablespoons (45 to 60 ml) water, as needed

Once the vegetables are in the oven, make the tahini sauce: In a small bowl, whisk together the tahini, lemon juice, garlic and salt to a small bowl until combined, then drizzle in the water and mix until smooth and pourable. Set aside until needed.

When the veggies have about 10 minutes left, make the flatbreads: Transfer the lentils *and* their soaking liquid to a blender along with the onion and garlic powders, pepper, salt and lemon juice. Blend until completely smooth. The mixture should be frothy, a little thinner than pancake batter, and will be a pinkish color.

Heat a large nonstick pan over medium heat. Once hot (make sure it's hot before adding the batter), pour about ½ cup (120 ml) of the batter onto the pan and swirl around the pan so the batter is about 7 inches (18 cm) in diameter. Cook over low to medium heat for 2 to 3 minutes, or until tiny bubbles form across the flatbread and the center looks dry. Be patient; sometimes the first flatbread is the most challenging. Using a thin silicone spatula, flip and cook for another minute. If the flatbread sticks, leave it for a little longer and then gradually wedge the spatula under the flatbread until it loosens. Once cooked, the flatbread will release from the pan. Transfer the flatbread to a plate and cover it to keep it warm. Repeat with the remaining batter.

Top each flatbread with roasted veggies, a sprinkle of arugula and some sliced avocado, and drizzle with tahini sauce.

MAPLE BAKON CAULIFLOWER STEAKS WITH LENTILS AND RANCH DRESSING

MAKES 3 SERVINGS NUT-FREE

MAPLE BAKON MARINADE

1 tbsp (7 g) smoked paprika

1 tbsp (4 g) nutritional yeast

1½ tsp (5 g) garlic powder

1½ tsp (4 g) onion powder

2 tbsp (30 ml) tamari

1 tbsp (15 ml) pure maple syrup

3 tbsp (45 ml) water

CAULIFLOWER STEAKS AND LENTILS

1 large head cauliflower

6 cups (180 g) baby spinach

1 large clove garlic, thinly sliced

2 cups (396 g) cooked or canned green or brown lentils, drained and rinsed

1 tbsp (15 ml) fresh lemon juice

Sea salt and freshly ground black pepper

Cauliflower continues to be a true whole food chameleon. While I love a whole roasted cauliflower, a steak is a more manageable means of allowing cauliflower the lead role on the plate. Here the salty and sweet cauliflower is served on a bed of tender lentils and bright greens, then topped with a zesty ranch-inspired sauce. It's a little impressive and a lot delicious. I can usually get three good steaks from a head of cauliflower, but I have two heads on hand in case the first is finicky.

Line a baking sheet with parchment paper and preheat the oven to 425°F (220°C).

Make the maple bakon marinade: In a small bowl, whisk together the paprika, nutritional yeast, garlic and onion powders, tamari, maple syrup and water.

Now, prepare the cauliflower: Cut off and discard the cauliflower leaves, being careful to keep as much of the base intact so that the cauliflower steaks stay together.

Set the cauliflower upright on a cutting board and cut it into 1-inch (2.5-cm)-thick steaks. Only the parts connected to the base will likely stay intact. I can usually get three steaks from a large cauliflower and then the ends fall apart. This is okay! The crumbly bits that fall apart can also be coated in marinade and roasted.

Lay the steaks flat on the prepared pan and, using a basting brush, brush the marinade all over the steaks (the side facing upward) and all loose florets, reserving a little more than 1 tablespoon (15 ml). Roast the steaks for 15 minutes.

After 15 minutes, remove the steaks from the oven and then baste the steaks and florets again with the remaining marinade. I prefer not to flip the steaks as this usually encourages some to fall apart. Return them to the oven for another 10 to 15 minutes, or until the steaks are fork tender and starting to brown on the edges.

RANCH DRESSING

½ cup (70 g) raw cashews, soaked in hot water for 1 hour

2 tbsp (8 g) hemp seeds

1½ tsp (5 g) garlic powder

1½ tsp (2 g) dried dill

2 tsp (7 g) dehydrated minced onion

1 tsp dried parsley

¼ tsp red pepper flakes, or to your preference

½ tsp sea salt or to taste

2 tbsp (30 ml) white wine vinegar

2 tbsp (30 ml) fresh lemon juice

½ cup (120 ml) water, plus more as needed

OPTIONAL GARNISH

Fresh herbs, such as flat-leaf parsley or dill, chopped

While the cauliflower is in the oven, make the ranch dressing: Drain the cashews, discarding the soaking liquid, and place them and the hemp seeds, garlic powder, dill, dehydrated onion, parsley, red pepper flakes, salt, vinegar, lemon juice and water in a blender. Blend on high speed until smooth. Add more water, a couple of tablespoons (about 30 ml) at a time, if needed, to reach a smooth consistency. You want it thick but easily pourable. Set aside.

When there's about 10 minutes left on the steaks, start the lentils: In a large sauté pan, sauté the spinach and garlic in a few tablespoons (about 30 ml) of a water for a minute. Now, add the lentils and cook over medium heat, stirring, until heated throughout and the spinach is wilted. Add the lemon juice and a pinch of salt and a few grinds of black pepper. Turn off the heat.

Divide the lentil mixture among the three plates and lay a maple bakon cauliflower steak on top. Drizzle with ranch dressing and garnish with fresh herbs.

> ### NOTES
>
> *Keep the ranch dressing in a glass container in the fridge for 3 to 5 days. It will thicken in the fridge; stir in some extra water to thin before serving.*
>
> *For a nut-free option, use sunflower seeds instead of cashews in the ranch dressing.*

SWEET ENDINGS: IRRESISTIBLE DESSERTS AND TREATS

I considered making this the first chapter; it's so exciting! Here the most delicious desserts are made from healthy whole foods—I get giddy even talking about it. I love a sweet treat, I especially love chocolate anything, but most vegan desserts are usually made with a lot of coconut oil, so I'm always dreaming up and working on something on the sweets continuum to meet my own dietary needs.

I'm confident that these desserts can compete with any traditional ones made from dairy, refined flours, oil or white sugar. I love to serve one of my no-bake cheesecakes (pages 161) to dinner guests and I always keep the Double Chocolate Chip Chickpea Cookies (page 164) and Fudgy Beet Brownies (page 184) in my freezer for those days when chocolate is just essential. You'll notice that these recipes also make use of everything from vegetables to beans, literally rewriting the book on how to make dessert.

SESAME MAPLE APPLE CRUMBLE

MAKES 6 SERVINGS ⊛ NUT-FREE OPTION

APPLE FILLING

1 lemon, halved

2¼ lb (1 kg) apples (about 5 apples;
I like Fuji apples for this recipe)

1 tbsp (9 g) arrowroot starch

¼ cup + 2 tbsp (56 g) coconut
sugar

½ tsp ground cinnamon

Pinch of sea salt

CRUMBLE

¼ cup (25 g) gluten-free oat flour

¼ cup (40 g) brown rice flour

1¼ cups (120 g) gluten-free old-
fashioned rolled oats

1 tsp baking powder

¼ tsp ground cinnamon

¼ tsp sea salt

⅓ cup (80 ml) pure maple syrup

⅓ cup (80 g) stirred tahini

2 tbsp (30 ml) unsweetened
almond or organic soy milk

Tahini and maple syrup make for an exceptional duo; it's a flavor pairing I cannot get enough of! Here, they take center stage in this easy and contemporary rendition of apple crumble. The oat topping is more chewy than crunchy, and the apple filling is mellow with notes of cinnamon and caramel. It's a moreish and warming dish that I've made for dinner guests but also just for myself when I'm craving a homemade dessert, especially in the colder months. Served alongside a scoop of vegan vanilla ice cream, it's downright divine. Be sure to thinly slice the apples for even baking.

Preheat the oven to 350°F (180°C).

Start the apple filling: Fill a large bowl with water and add the juice from one lemon half. Peel your apples and cut them into ⅛-inch (3-mm)-thick slices. Place the apple slices in the lemon water until needed. This keeps them from browning while you prepare the rest of the crumble.

Begin the crumble: In a medium-sized bowl, mix together the oat and rice flours, oats, baking powder, cinnamon and salt.

In a separate small bowl, whisk together the maple syrup, tahini and milk until smooth. Pour this mixture into the bowl of dry ingredients and mix until no dry spots remain. Set aside.

Drain the apples well and transfer them to a 7 x 11-inch (18 x 28-cm) casserole dish (or similar size). Squeeze the other lemon half over the apples and sprinkle with the arrowroot starch, coconut sugar, cinnamon and salt. Toss well to coat all the apple slices evenly.

Using damp hands, drop bits of crumble all over the apples and press it together so the top is evenly covered. It will be a little sticky.

Cover the dish tightly with tinfoil and bake for 50 minutes, then remove the tinfoil and bake for another 5 minutes. You can even pop it under a broiler for a minute or two if you want to get more color on the top.

Remove the crumble from the oven and let it rest for 5 minutes. Spoon the crumble into bowls and serve as is or with a dollop of vegan yogurt or scoop of dairy-free ice cream.

PEANUT BUTTER CARAMEL COOKIE SANDWICHES

MAKES 14 COOKIE SANDWICHES (28 COOKIES)

COOKIES

2 cups (192 g) gluten-free old-fashioned rolled oats, divided

⅓ cup (50 g) coconut sugar

1 tsp baking powder

½ tsp baking soda

¼ tsp ground cinnamon

¼ tsp sea salt

½ cup (70 g) raw cashews, soaked in hot water for 1 to 3 hours

½ cup (120 ml) unsweetened almond milk or organic soy milk

⅓ cup (80 ml) pure maple syrup

2 tsp (10 ml) pure vanilla extract

1 cup (182 g) cooked or canned navy beans, drained and rinsed

These revolutionary cookies are made from oats, nuts and *beans*! They're so good, it feels wrong. I practically jumped for joy when I took my first bite. The beans create an unbelievably light texture while offering fiber, protein and iron. With the perfect ratio of ooey-gooey caramel (made from dates and peanut butter) to chewy cookie, it'll be hard to resist eating two. Or three. Juicy, creamy dates are essential for the caramel, and I highly recommend using a ¾-ounce cookie scoop (about 2 tablespoons [30 ml]) to scoop and shape your cookies.

Preheat the oven to 350°F (180°C) and line a large baking sheet with parchment paper.

First, make the cookies: In a large bowl, stir together 1 cup (96 g) of the oats, the coconut sugar, baking powder, baking soda, cinnamon and salt. Set aside.

Drain the cashews, discarding the soaking liquid, and place them, the remaining cup (96 g) of oats, milk, maple syrup, vanilla and navy beans in a high-speed blender. Blend on high speed, using your tamper to assist the blending, until completely smooth. The mixture will be thick.

Add the blender batter to the bowl of dry ingredients and mix until no dry spots remain. The consistency will be a little loose but not watery. Clean the blender; you'll use it again.

Using a ¾-ounce cookie scoop (about 2 tablespoons [30 ml]), scoop out the dough, and transfer it to the pan, keeping about 1 inch (2.5 cm) between each cookie. The batter will be loose enough to relax into a 2-inch (5-cm)-wide cookie.

(continued)

PEANUT BUTTER CARAMEL COOKIE SANDWICHES
(CONTINUED)

DATE CARAMEL

1 cup (178 g) pitted, soft and juicy Medjool or Deglet Noor dates

¼ cup (64 g) stirred all-natural peanut butter

¼ tsp sea salt

⅓ cup (80 ml) unsweetened almond milk or organic soy milk, plus more as needed

Bake for 12 to 14 minutes, or until the cookies are slightly firm. Remove the cookies from the oven and let them cool on the pan for 10 minutes. Then, using a thin spatula, gently transfer them to a cooling rack and let cool completely. The cookies will set as they cool.

While the cookies are baking, make the caramel: In a high-speed blender or food processor, combine the dates, peanut butter, salt and milk, double checking as you go that all the pits are removed from the dates!

Start blending on low speed and increase to high and blend or process until smooth and creamy, using a tamper to assist the blending if using a high-speed blender. Add more milk, 1 tablespoon (15 ml) at a time, if needed, to achieve a smooth consistency. Too much milk will make the caramel too loose, so add only what's needed. The caramel should be stiff but soft and easily stick to a spoon without dripping.

Once the cookies are cool, assemble your sandwiches: Spoon 1 tablespoon (15 ml) of the caramel onto the bottom of one cookie and top with another cookie so that the flat bottoms are facing inward. Continue until all the cookie sandwiches are filled.

You can keep these cookies in a covered container for up to 3 days in the fridge or freeze (caramel and all) for up to 3 months. I like to use any leftover caramel as a dip for sliced apples.

> ### NOTES
>
> *You can substitute another nut butter for peanut butter, if you prefer.*
>
> *If your dates are dry, soak them in water for 30 minutes first and drain well before using..*

MINT CHOCOLATE ICE CREAM CHEESECAKE

MAKES 12 TO 16 SLICES

CRUST

¾ cup (109 g) almonds

¾ cup (75 g) walnuts

1 cup (96 g) gluten-free old-fashioned rolled oats

1¼ cups (223 g) pitted juicy Medjool or Deglet Noor dates

1 tsp pure vanilla extract

½ tsp sea salt

1 tbsp (15 ml) unsweetened almond milk or organic soy milk, plus more if needed

You know that sigh of satisfaction after the first bite? This cake will make you do that. It's simply wonderful and made without any added sugar. It's a cross between cheesecake and ice cream cake—rich and smooth, cold and creamy—and it's surprisingly easy to make. You can dig in when it's still a little frozen or let it rest longer once out of the freezer and it will yield somewhere between ice cream and mousse. I like to add the eye-catching swirl, but you can skip it and make a more basic, still outrageously yummy, version if you prefer (see Notes). You can also customize this cake by pressing chopped nuts or vegan chocolate chips into the surface. If you're not a big fan of peppermint, skip the extract and go with a straight chocolate option.

Line an 8-inch (20.5-cm) round springform pan with parchment paper by tracing the bottom of the pan onto parchment. Cut it out and fit it into the pan.

Make the crust: In a food processor, combine the almonds, walnuts, oats, dates, vanilla, salt and milk, and process continuously until there are no large chunks of dates or nuts and the mixture starts to clump together and easily sticks together when pressed between your fingers. If the crust isn't coming together, add an additional tablespoon of the milk and continue to process again.

Transfer the mixture to the prepared springform pan and press it evenly and firmly into the bottom of the pan, working from the middle outward to the edges of the pan. Place the pan in the fridge until the filling is ready.

(continued)

FILLING

2 cups (280 g) raw cashews, soaked in hot water for 1 to 3 hours

1 cup (240 ml) unsweetened almond or organic soy milk

1 tsp peppermint extract

¼ tsp sea salt

¾ cup (134 g) pitted, juicy Medjool or Deglet Noor dates

¼ cup (22 g) unsweetened cocoa powder

2 tsp (10 ml) pure vanilla extract

Now make the filling: Add the cashews, milk, peppermint extract and salt to a high speed blender and blend on high until smooth, using your tamper to assist the blending. Remove 3 tablespoons (45 ml) of the blended mixture and set aside. Then, add the dates, cocoa powder and vanilla to the blender (with the already blended portion) and blend again on high speed until completely smooth.

Pour this blended mixture into the crust and use an offset spatula or spoon to evenly spread the filling.

Drop small spoonfuls of the reserved white filling over the top, then drag a sharp knife through the cheesecake, making a swirl pattern.

Place the cake on a level surface in the freezer and freeze it for at least 6 hours. Overnight is ideal.

Remove the cheesecake from the freezer and immediately run a butter knife or thin spatula around the edge of the pan to release it. As soon as you remove the cake from the pan, carefully peel the parchment paper off the bottom of the cake. Transfer the cake to a cutting board or serving plate and cut into slices, using a sharp knife, wiping the knife clean between cuts for best results. Wait 5 to 10 minutes and serve—it will be like ice cream cake—or wait 30 to 40 minutes for the cake to soften if you want more of a cheesecake texture.

NOTES

If your dates for the filling are hard or dry, soak them in the almond milk for 30 minutes before adding both to the blender.

If you want to skip the marbled effect, make the filling as follows. Drain the cashews, discarding the soaking liquid. Add them and all the other filling ingredients to a high-speed blender and blend on high speed until completely smooth. Pour the mixture into the crust. Use an offset spatula or back of a spoon to spread the filling and continue with the recipe as written.

DOUBLE CHOCOLATE CHIP CHICKPEA COOKIES

MAKES 12 COOKIES NUT-FREE

WET INGREDIENTS

1½ tsp (3 g) whole psyllium husk

¼ cup (60 ml) water

⅓ cup (85 g) stirred sunflower seed butter (see page 23 on how to make your own)

⅓ cup (80 ml) pure maple syrup

DRY INGREDIENTS

1 cup (120 g) chickpea flour

⅓ cup (50 g) coconut sugar

¼ cup (22 g) unsweetened cocoa powder

¾ tsp baking powder

½ tsp sea salt

½ cup (88 g) mini vegan chocolate chips, if desired

I had a chocolate chip chickpea cookie at one of my favorite vegan cafés and I was instantly hooked. The following week I baked batch after batch until I was equally in love with my own version. And this is that finalized cookie! It's everything you might want from a cozy cookie—indulgent, chewy, rich, delicious. I made it double chocolate to satisfy any chocolate cravings and since it's made with chickpea flour, it's also full of plant-based protein. I like to serve these warm while they're still soft. A tall glass of cold soy milk isn't a bad idea either. Note here that it's best to hold off on licking the spoon or eating the raw cookie dough—uncooked chickpea flour tastes terrible. It's also easier to scoop and shape the stiff dough if you have a spring release cookie scoop (here, I use a 1.25-ounce cookie scoop [about 2.5 tablespoons (37 ml)]). These are also nut-free, meaning they're lunchbox appropriate!

Preheat the oven to 350°F (180°C) and line a large baking sheet with parchment paper.

Start with the wet ingredients: In a medium-sized bowl, whisk together the psyllium husk and water, and set the mixture aside for 5 minutes to thicken.

Meanwhile, in a large bowl, combine the chickpea flour, coconut sugar, cocoa powder, baking powder and salt.

Once the psyllium mixture has thickened, add the sunflower seed butter and maple syrup to the psyllium bowl and whisk together until smooth and combined.

Add the wet mixture to the dry mixture and mix until no dry spots remain. The dough will be stiff, thick and sticky. Fold in the chocolate chips.

(continued)

DOUBLE CHOCOLATE CHIP CHICKPEA COOKIES (CONTINUED)

Using a 1.25-ounce cookie scoop (about 2½ tablespoons [37 ml]), scoop the dough right onto the prepared pan, keeping at least 1½ inches (4 cm) between cookies. Dampen your hands and gently press the surface of the cookies so they're about 2½ inches (6.5 cm) in diameter. Shape the edges with your fingers to get a nice, rounded cookie.

Bake for 12 to 13 minutes, or until the edges are firm and the center looks dry. Remove the cookies from the oven, place the pan on a cooling rack and let the cookies cool for 15 minutes. Then, using a thin spatula, remove them from the pan and place them on a serving plate. The bottoms of the cookies might leave a little residue on the parchment paper after they've been lifted from the pan; this is normal.

Keep these cookies in a sealed container on the counter for a couple of days, in the fridge for up to 5 days or in the freezer for up to 3 months. If you keep the cookies in the fridge, they'll firm up. If you want to soften them, pop them in a preheated oven (around 350°F [180°C]) for a few minutes or give them a quick warm-up for 10 to 20 seconds in a microwave.

NOTES

If you want to skip the chocolate chips, you can use cacao nibs or any nut or seed.

If you don't have sunflower seed butter, you can use almond butter or all-natural peanut butter, which will also impact the flavor but will still taste great.

MOLASSES GINGERBREAD LOAF WITH BUTTERCREAM ICING

GINGERBREAD

4 tsp (7 g) whole psyllium husk

½ cup (120 ml) water

2 cups (200 g) gluten-free oat flour

1¼ cups (120 g) blanched almond flour

⅓ cup (50 g) coconut sugar

1 tbsp (14 g) baking powder

1 tsp baking soda

2 tsp (5 g) ground cinnamon

1½ tsp (3 g) ground ginger

½ tsp ground cloves

¼ tsp ground nutmeg

¼ tsp sea salt

¼ cup (60 ml) blackstrap or unsulfured molasses

Zest of 1 large orange

3 tbsp (45 ml) fresh orange juice

2 tsp (10 ml) pure vanilla extract

1 cup (240 ml) unsweetened almond milk or organic soy milk

This cozy gingerbread could be a recipe that gets passed down from generation to generation—it has an old-fashioned feel. Warming spices, orange zest and molasses create deep flavor, and when glazed with rich and creamy icing, it's nothing but irresistible. You can make the gingerbread ahead of time and freeze it once it's cooled, but I do suggest making the icing within a couple of days of serving. I never miss the opportunity to slice this loaf at the table, either; it's too beautiful to keep hidden in the kitchen. I like to soak the cashews a little longer for the buttercream icing to ensure it's silky smooth.

Adjust the oven rack to the middle of the oven and preheat to 350°F (180°C). Line a standard loaf pan (8½ x 4½ x 2½ inches [21.5 x 11.5 x 6.5 cm]) with parchment paper so that the parchment hangs out over the longer opposing sides.

Make the gingerbread: In a small bowl, mix together the psyllium and the water, and set it aside for 5 minutes to thicken.

In a large bowl, combine the oat and almond flours, coconut sugar, baking powder, baking soda, cinnamon, ginger, cloves, nutmeg and salt, and mix well, making sure to break up any clumps of almond flour or coconut sugar.

In a blender, combine the molasses, orange zest and juice, vanilla and milk, and blend until smooth.

Add the blended mixture and thickened psyllium husk to the bowl of dry ingredients and mix until no dry spots remain. Transfer the batter to the prepared pan. Bake for 50 to 60 minutes. The loaf is done when it's firm to the touch in the center and the edges have pulled away from the pan.

(continued)

BUTTERCREAM ICING

1 cup (140 g) raw cashews, soaked in hot water for 3 hours

Juice of ½ lemon

¼ cup (60 ml) agave syrup

¼ cup (60 ml) unsweetened almond or organic soy milk, plus more if needed

¼ tsp sea salt

OPTIONAL GARNISHES

½ cup (73 g) chopped almonds

¾ cup (109 g) fresh blueberries, whole or halved

Remove the loaf from the oven and let it cool in the pan for 30 minutes. Slide a thin spatula or butter knife along the sides of the loaf that are touching the pan to release any stuck-on parts. Then, remove the loaf from the pan by pulling up on the parchment, transfer to a cooling rack and let it cool completely.

While the loaf is in the oven, make the icing: Drain the cashews, discarding the soaking liquid, and place them in a high-speed blender with the lemon juice, agave, milk and salt. Blend on high speed, using your tamper to assist the blending, until completely smooth. Add more milk, 1 tablespoon (15 ml) at a time, if needed, to assist the blending, until a creamy texture is reached. Transfer the icing to a container and cover. Place in the fridge to set.

When the cake has cooled, spoon the icing over the top. Garnish with chopped almonds and berries and slice into eight slices, wiping the knife between slices for best results.

NOTES

Psyllium husk is soluble fiber that turns into a gel when mixed with water or another liquid. It works like a binder in baked goods and can be used to replace eggs and oil. You can find whole psyllium husk in most health food stores and in the organic aisle in many grocery stores.

I use whole psyllium husk but you can also use psyllium powder. In general, 3 teaspoons of whole psyllium husk is equal to 2.5 teaspoons of psyllium powder.

THE CHOCOLATE CUPCAKE

MAKES 12 CUPCAKES

CUPCAKES

2 tbsp (10 g) whole psyllium husk

½ cup (120 ml) water

¾ cup (72 g) blanched almond flour

¾ cup (90 g) buckwheat flour

¾ cup (108 g) coconut sugar

⅓ cup (29 g) unsweetened cocoa powder

3 tbsp (27 g) arrowroot starch

1½ tsp (7 g) baking powder

½ tsp baking soda

¼ tsp sea salt

1 cup (240 ml) unsweetened almond milk or organic soy milk

¼ cup (60 ml) pure maple syrup

¼ cup (64 g) stirred almond butter, all-natural peanut butter or sunflower seed butter

1½ tsp (8 ml) apple cider vinegar

These cupcakes have "indulgence" written all over them. From the decadent cupcakes to the whipped frosting, they're unbelievably delicious. Over the last decade (yes, decade!), I've tried more times than I can count to create a healthy vegan and gluten-free cupcake, without using vegetable oil, confectioners' sugar or refined flours, which still lived up to cupcake hype. It sounds like a tall order, doesn't it? It required some interesting trial and error, but this chocolate cupcake is THE cupcake! The frosting, thick enough that you can pipe it, is gloriously made with chickpeas, debunking the notion that frosting is just sugar. I turn to this recipe when I want to serve a special treat or when a single-serving celebratory dessert is called for. I usually use almond butter or sunflower seed butter in these cupcakes, but you can try peanut butter if you want a chocolate-peanut butter flavor.

First, make the cupcakes: Adjust the oven rack to the middle of the oven and preheat to 350°F (180°C).

In a small bowl, mix together the psyllium husk and water, and set aside for 5 minutes to thicken.

In a large bowl, mix together the almond and buckwheat flours, coconut sugar, cocoa powder, arrowroot starch, baking powder, baking soda and salt. Set aside.

In a blender, combine the almond milk, maple syrup, almond butter and vinegar, and blend until smooth.

Create a well in the middle of the bowl of dry ingredients and pour in the blended mixture, followed by the thickened psyllium mixture. Mix with a large spoon or spatula until no dry spots remain.

If not using a nonstick muffin tin, place a muffin wrapper into each muffin well.

(continued)

CHOCOLATE FROSTING

1½ cups (255 g) cooked or canned chickpeas, drained and rinsed

6 tbsp (32 g) unsweetened cocoa powder

½ cup (120 ml) pure maple syrup

¼ cup (64 g) stirred almond butter

¼ tsp sea salt

¾ tsp pure vanilla extract

Almond milk, if needed

Fill each muffin well with batter until two-thirds full. Bake for 20 to 22 minutes. The cupcakes are done when they've pulled away from the tin and are slightly firm to the touch. Remove the cupcakes from the oven and let them cool for 10 minutes in the muffin pan, then transfer them to a cooling rack to cool completely.

While the cupcakes are cooling, make the frosting: In a high-speed blender, combine the chickpeas, cocoa powder, maple syrup, almond butter, salt and vanilla, and blend until completely smooth. If you want a looser consistency, add almond milk, a couple of teaspoons (about 10 ml) at a time, and blend again. Transfer the frosting to a bowl or container and cover. Place the frosting in the fridge until needed.

When you're ready to frost your cupcakes, you can transfer the frosting to a piping bag and pipe it onto the cupcakes, or just smear it onto each one with an offset spatula.

Keep the cupcakes in the fridge for up to 3 days or in the freezer (frosting and all) for up to 3 months.

> NOTE
>
> *If making the frosting ahead of time, note that it will become stiffer in the fridge. Let it come to room temperature before using and feel free to add a little more almond milk to loosen.*

NEAPOLITAN ICE CREAM LOAF CAKE

CRUST

1 cup (100 g) walnuts

½ cup packed (95 g) pitted juicy Medjool or Deglet Noor dates

3 tbsp (16 g) unsweetened cocoa powder

1 tsp pure vanilla extract

¼ tsp sea salt

1 tbsp (15 ml) unsweetened almond milk or organic soy milk

⅓ cup (48 g) cacao nibs or (58 g) mini vegan chocolate chips

FILLING

2 cups (280 g) raw cashews, soaked in hot water for 1 to 3 hours

½ cup (120 ml) unsweetened almond milk or organic soy milk

⅓ cup (80 ml) pure maple syrup

1 tbsp (15 ml) fresh lemon juice

½ tsp pure vanilla extract

¼ tsp ground cinnamon

Pinch of sea salt

¼ cup (56 g) peeled and roughly chopped raw purple beet

Traditional and modern merge in this luxurious ice cream cake conveniently made in a loaf pan. It's the type of dessert you're excited to serve guests—it shouts "homemade gourmet" but is rather easy to make. Neapolitan-inspired cashew "ice cream" is layered on top of a chocolaty walnut crust. It's as pretty as it is delicious and it's rich without being heavy. Raw beets act as a clever food coloring and it's what I consider a showstopping dessert. Give it a few minutes to soften once it's removed from the freezer, but also note that when it's left on the counter for a little longer to thaw, it has the texture of a soft and creamy semifreddo.

Line a standard loaf pan (8½ x 4½ x 2½ inches [21.5 x 11.5 x 6.5 cm]) with parchment paper so that the parchment hangs out over the opposing long sides of the pan.

Start with the crust: In a food processor, combine the walnuts, dates, cocoa powder, vanilla, salt and milk, and process until the mixture easily sticks together when pressed between your fingers and no large chunks of dates or nuts remain. Add the cacao nibs and pulse until combined.

Remove the crust from the food processor and transfer it to the prepared pan. Press the crust evenly into the bottom of the pan. Place the pan in the fridge.

Make the filling: Drain the cashews and discard the soaking water. Place them and the milk, maple syrup, lemon juice, vanilla, cinnamon and salt in a high-speed blender, and blend until completely smooth. Use your tamper to assist the blending. This is the white, or vanilla, layer.

(continued)

NEAPOLITAN ICE CREAM LOAF CAKE
(CONTINUED)

Remove the loaf pan from the fridge and pour about half the white cashew filling into the crust. Spread this layer with a silicone spatula.

Remove 1 heaping tablespoon (about 20 ml) of the filling from the white mixture remaining in the blender and set it aside. You'll use this later to create a swirl effect on the top of the cake.

Now, add the chopped beets to the filling in the blender and blend again until completely smooth. This is the pink layer.

Pour the pink layer on top of the white layer, again using a silicone spatula to gently spread the layer until it's even.

Next, drop the reserved white filling by ½ teaspoons randomly over the top of the beet layer and drag a sharp knife through the drops, creating a swirl effect. Place the ice cream cake on a level surface in the freezer and freeze for 6 hours or overnight.

When ready to serve, remove the cake from the freezer. Gently slide a butter knife or thin spatula between the cake and the loaf pan on the short edge of the pan to release it. Lift the cake out of the loaf pan by pulling on the overhanging parchment paper. Use a clean, sharp knife to cut the cheesecake into 10 slices, wiping the knife between each slice. If freezing the cake overnight or longer, remove it from the freezer 10 to 15 minutes before serving.

BLACK FOREST CAKE CHIA PUDDING PARFAIT

MAKES 5 LARGE PARFAITS

5 chocolate cupcakes (without icing), from The Chocolate Cupcake recipe (page 170)

15 fresh cherries, pitted and quartered

2 tbsp (18 g) cacao nibs or (22 g) vegan chocolate chips (optional)

CHIA PUDDING

½ cup (70 g) raw cashews, soaked in hot water for 1 to 3 hours

3 tbsp (45 ml) pure maple syrup

Pinch of sea salt

½ tsp pure vanilla extract

2 cups (475 ml) water

¼ cup +1 tbsp (51 g) chia seeds

½ cup (80 g) dried tart cherries, roughly chopped

This recipe was a serendipitous experiment. I had leftover cupcakes from The Chocolate Cupcake (page 170) and cashew chia pudding in my fridge. My sweet tooth was calling, and I was inspired to mix things up, literally. What transpired hit the spot! Cakey, creamy and reminiscent of a chocolate English trifle, this parfait is one of my favorite desserts, ever. Tart, fresh cherries kick the flavor up a notch, but if fresh aren't available, you can easily omit them. I plan for this dessert whenever I make the cupcakes by setting aside five after they've cooled. Either freeze the cupcakes (without the icing) for later or keep them in the fridge for a day or two, until needed.

First, prepare the cupcakes as written on page 170: Either make them and let them cool, or take them out of the freezer and let them defrost completely on the counter or in the fridge. You don't need the icing, just the cupcakes.

Meanwhile, make the chia pudding: Drain the cashews, discarding the soaking liquid, and place them in a high-speed blender along with maple syrup, salt, vanilla and water. Blend on high speed for a minute, or until silky smooth. Transfer the cashew mixture to a container with a lid and add the chia seeds and dried cherries. Cover, then shake every couple of minutes for 5 to 10 minutes. This keeps the chia seeds from clumping at the bottom. Then, place the pudding in the fridge overnight or for at least 3 hours. Shake or mix every now and then, if possible, for the first hour.

Once the chia pudding is ready, assemble the parfaits: You'll use one cupcake for each parfait. Tear up the cupcakes into bite-sized pieces. Place half of a cupcake in the bottom of each glass, followed by about ¼ cup (60 ml) of chia pudding. Top with the other half of the cupcake and then another ¼ cup (60 ml) of chia pudding. Garnish with fresh cherries and cacao nibs. Place the parfaits in the fridge to set for at least 30 minutes and up to 8 hours before serving.

CHAMELEON COOKIE DOUGH

MAKES 2 PACKED CUPS (490 G)

1 cup (170 g) cooked or canned chickpeas, drained and rinsed

1 cup (96 g) blanched almond flour

⅓ cup (85 g) stirred almond butter or all-natural peanut butter

¼ cup (60 ml) pure maple syrup

2 tbsp (18 g) coconut sugar

2 tsp (10 ml) pure vanilla extract

Pinch of ground cinnamon

¼ tsp sea salt

½ cup (88 g) mini vegan chocolate chips

Cookie dough summons childhood nostalgia for many of us, me included, and I knew I wanted a versatile, plant-based, copycat cookie dough for this book. After many iterations, this finalized version hits the spot! I like to steal a spoonful when I want something sweet, but since I also know I'm getting protein and fiber, it feels less like a sweet tooth–driven snack and more like a nutritious treat.

In a food processor, combine the chickpeas, almond flour, almond butter, maple syrup, coconut sugar, vanilla, cinnamon, and salt, and process until smooth. Scrape down the sides and process again. It will be thick. Add the chocolate chips and pulse until incorporated. Spoon the cookie dough into a bowl and set in the fridge, covered, until needed. You can keep this cookie dough in the fridge for up to 5 days or in the freezer for up to 3 months.

NOTES

If vegan chocolate chips aren't in your diet, try cacao nibs, raisins or dried cranberries in the cookie dough.

The sweetness of the cookie dough will depend on which brand of chocolate chips you use. For a less sweet cookie dough, you can omit the coconut sugar or reduce the maple syrup.

COOKIE DOUGH TWO WAYS

Cookie Dough Balls: Preheat the oven to 350°F (180°C). Scoop out about 2 tablespoons (30 g) of cookie dough and, using damp hands, roll it into a ball and place it on a parchment-lined baking sheet. Repeat with the remaining cookie dough. Bake for 20 to 22 minutes for soft cookies, or 25 to 26 minutes for firmer cookies. Remove from the oven and let cool.

Cookie Dough Nice Cream: In a high-speed blender, combine 4 large peeled and sliced frozen bananas with just a splash of milk and blend on high speed, using the blender's tamper to push the bananas into the blade, until you get a creamy banana nice cream. Transfer the banana nice cream to a bowl and stir in chunks of the cookie dough (as much as you want).

TWO-BITE COOKIE DOUGH SQUARES

1 batch Chameleon Cookie Dough
(page 179)

COOKIE CRUST

1½ tsp (3 g) whole psyllium husk

¼ cup (60 ml) water

2 tbsp (30 ml) pure maple syrup

1 cup (96 g) blanched almond flour

⅔ cup (66 g) gluten-free oat flour

¼ tsp ground cinnamon

½ tsp sea salt

You can easily turn Chameleon Cookie Dough (page 179) into a square! Here, the chickpea-based cookie dough is layered on top of a light almond crust and baked until set. These are a perfect little snack served alongside tea or coffee and are great right out of the freezer.

First, make your cookie dough according to the recipe on page 179 and set in the fridge, covered, until needed.

Preheat the oven to 350°F (180°C) and line an 8-inch (20.5-cm) square baking pan with parchment paper so that the parchment is hanging out over two opposing sides.

Make the cookie crust: In a small bowl, mix together the psyllium husk, water and maple syrup. Set aside for 5 minutes to thicken.

In a separate medium-sized bowl, mix together the almond and oat flours, cinnamon and salt. Pour the thickened psyllium mixture into the dry ingredients and, using a spatula or even your hands, mix until everything is combined and no dry spots remain.

With slightly damp hands, press the dough evenly into the prepared baking pan. Bake the crust for 10 minutes. After 10 minutes, remove it from the oven.

Now, drop spoonfuls of the cookie dough over the crust and work it together with your hands (be careful, the pan will be hot). Press it into the pan so it's even. Again, you can do this with damp hands to prevent sticking.

Return the pan to the oven for another 20 to 22 minutes, or until the cookie dough looks dry and is firm to the touch. Remove the cookie dough from the oven and let it cool completely on a cooling rack, then place the pan in the fridge to let the squares set for 1 to 3 hours.

Remove the pan from the fridge and take the cookie dough from the pan by pulling up on the parchment paper. Using a sharp knife, cut the dough into 16 squares, wiping your knife between cuts to get clean slices.

You can keep these cookie dough squares in the fridge for 3 days or in the freezer for up to 3 months.

CHOCOLATE PUDDING THREE WAYS

MAKES 4 SERVINGS (WITH LEFTOVER ALMOND CACAO CRUMBLE)

PUDDING

1 medium-sized ripe avocado, pitted and peeled, OR 1 cup (140 g) raw cashews, soaked in hot water for 1 hour, OR 1 (12-oz [340-g]) package extra-firm silken tofu (see Notes)

1 large ripe banana

½ cup (120 ml) unsweetened almond or organic soy milk (omit if using silken tofu)

⅓ cup (60 g) pitted juicy Medjool or Deglet Noor dates

¼ cup (22 g) unsweetened cocoa powder

Pinch of sea salt

ALMOND CACAO CRUMBLE

¾ cup (109 g) almonds

1 cup (96 g) old-fashioned gluten-free rolled oats

3 tbsp (27 g) coconut sugar

3 tbsp (33 g) hemp seeds

½ tsp sea salt

¼ tsp ground cinnamon

½ cup (72 g) cacao nibs or (88 g) mini vegan chocolate chips

GARNISH

1 cup (140 to 150 g) fresh berries

Chocolate pudding was a staple snack when I was a kid, and this version is a little more grown-up and considerably more nutritious. The Almond Cacao Crumble is an optional addition, but it adds depth and deliciousness to this pudding—I highly suggest trying it. And it's multipurpose—you can also sprinkle it on oatmeal, chia pudding or any sweet, blended concoction.

Make the pudding: First, pick your base—avocado, cashews or tofu—and place it in a blender (be sure to drain the cashews or tofu) with the banana, milk, dates, cocoa powder and salt, and blend until completely smooth. Remember to omit the milk if using silken tofu. Use the tamper to help blend. Transfer the pudding to a container or bowl and refrigerate for at least 1 hour. Let the pudding set in the fridge for at least 2 hours if using tofu.

Next, make the crumble: In a food processor, pulse the almonds until they're broken up. Then, add the oats, coconut sugar, hemp seeds, salt, cinnamon and cacao nibs, and pulse until the oats are coarsely ground. Transfer to a container with a cover. Keep covered in a cool, dry place for up to 1 month. Be sure to shake the crumble before using, to evenly distribute the delicious bits.

When it comes time to serve, spoon the pudding into bowls and sprinkle with 1 to 2 tablespoons (7 to 14 g) of the crumble, then toss in some berries. This pudding will keep in the fridge for up to 3 days.

> ### NOTES
>
> *If using cashews, soak them for 1 hour in hot water, then drain and continue with the recipe as written. You may need a little more almond milk to blend and reach a smooth consistency.*
>
> *If using silken tofu, drain the tofu and add to the blender with all the other ingredients. The tofu provides a lot of liquid, so omit the milk.*

SWEET ENDINGS: IRRESISTIBLE DESSERTS AND TREATS

FUDGY BEET BROWNIES

MAKES 12 TO 16 BROWNIES

10 oz (300 g) beets (2 small to medium-sized beets), scrubbed and chopped into 2″ (5-cm) chunks (2 cups chopped)

1 cup (97 g) chickpea flour

¾ cup (75 g) gluten-free oat flour

1 cup (144 g) coconut sugar

1 cup (86 g) unsweetened cocoa powder

2 tsp (9 g) baking powder

½ tsp sea salt

1 cup (100 g) walnuts, divided

1 tsp pure vanilla extract

¾ cup (175 ml) unsweetened almond milk or organic soy milk

½ cup (88 g) mini vegan chocolate chips, plus more for garnish if desired

Roasted beets do some heavy lifting in these rich and dense brownies. They add texture, moisture and a tempting red velvet hue without any of the earthy beet flavor you might anticipate. These are unquestionably unique and the most delicious brownies I've ever made. The dark bitter chocolate and sweet coconut sugar balance each other perfectly; and the chickpea flour and walnut base offers such essential nutrients as protein and omega-3 fatty acids without compromising any of the fudgy goodness you expect from a great brownie. These are at their best when cooled, but are also super yummy served a little warm with vegan ice cream.

First, roast the beets: Preheat the oven to 400°F (200°C). Remove any gnarly stems or thick-skinned areas from the beets. Place the beets in a small casserole dish and pour a little bit of water into the bottom of the dish, just enough to cover the bottom. Cover the dish tightly with tinfoil and roast the beets for 45 to 60 minutes. They're done when they're fork-tender. Remove the beets from the oven and keep the tinfoil on for 15 minutes so they continue to steam. Then, remove the foil and let cool completely. I like to turn the oven off at this point and come back to the brownies a few hours later. Once the beets are cooled, peel off the skins.

Start making the brownies: Preheat the oven to 350°F (180°C). Line an 8-inch (20.5-cm) square baking pan with parchment paper so that the parchment hangs out over two opposing sides.

In a large bowl, mix together the chickpea and oat flours, coconut sugar, cocoa powder, baking powder and salt. Be sure to break up any clumps of coconut sugar.

(continued)

Set aside ¼ cup (25 g) of the walnuts (we'll use these to garnish the brownies). In a high-speed blender, combine the remaining ¾ cup (75 g) of walnuts, vanilla, milk and roasted beets, and blend until completely smooth. It will resemble a hot pink milkshake.

Add the blended mixture to the bowl of dry ingredients and mix until well combined. The batter will be thick. Fold in the chocolate chips.

Transfer the batter to the prepared baking pan and smooth out the surface. Chop the reserved walnuts and scatter them over the top of the brownies, lightly pressing them into the batter. You can also sprinkle some additional chocolate chips on the surface, if desired. Bake for 27 to 30 minutes. The brownies are done when small cracks appear on the surface and the middle is just about firm.

Remove the brownies from the oven and let them cool completely in the pan on a cooling rack. Once cooled, lift the brownies out of the pan by pulling on the parchment paper, and transfer them to a cutting board. Cut into 12 to 16 brownies. These brownies are super fudgy, so be sure to wipe the knife clean with a damp cloth between each cut for nicely shaped brownies.

These will keep in the fridge in a tightly sealed container for up to 3 days. Otherwise, keep in the freezer for up to 3 months.

> NOTE
>
> *You can soak the walnuts for 4 to 6 hours for easier digestion and blending, if desired. Drain before using.*
>
> *If vegan chocolate chips aren't in your diet, omit.*

ACKNOWLEDGMENTS

First, my boys—Bernard and George. Thank you for your patience and willingness to eat cold food, leftovers and the same thing over and over until I got the recipe right. George, thank you for napping so I could run around the kitchen, quite literally, and for tolerating all our grocery store visits. Bernard, I'm so grateful for your never-ever-ending support and for pushing me when I don't feel motivated or inspired. I love you both and can't imagine my life and kitchen without you.

To my wonderful testers, I'm infinitely appreciative of all your hard work, communication and commitment. To Julie specifically, you're the best. I couldn't have reached the finish line without your help.

Jane, thank you for all your chopping and slicing and cleaning. You're the best sous chef and an important part of our family. Bernard, George and I are so lucky to have you.

To mom and dad, Penney and Pam, I couldn't have juggled this book, traveling home and being a mom without your love and reassurance. My heart is with you always.

To Dustin, you're ultimately the reason this cookbook exists, and I am ever grateful for your guidance, advice and friendship. And that we sat next to each other on that first day.

To Page Street and Marissa, it's been a wonderful experience to have partnered with you for this project and to now be a part of the Page Street family. Thank you for your understanding, direction and love of good food and support of passionate authors!

ABOUT THE AUTHOR

Ashley is a trained chef, certified holistic nutritionist, cookbook author and creator of RiseShineCook.ca. She left her career as a clinical pharmacist to pursue nutrition and the culinary arts after she was diagnosed with multiple sclerosis in her twenties. Ashley believes that eating more plant-based whole foods and fewer processed foods is one of the most important steps in preventing, and even healing from, chronic disease. Her first cookbook *The Plant-Based Cookbook: Vegan, Gluten-Free, Oil-Free Recipes For Lifelong Health* is listed as one of Amazon's Editor's Picks for Best Cookbooks and has been featured in *Forks Over Knives* magazine, *Vegan Food and Living* magazine and *VegNews*. Ashley currently lives in Taiwan with her husband, Bernard; son, George; and beloved collection of cookbooks.

INDEX

C

PLANT-BASED DELICIOUS

PLANT-BASED DELICIOUS